# DRILLING DOWN

*AND*

# LEVELING UP

Praise for **DRILLING DOWN** AND **LEVELING UP**: Attaining consistency, profitability, and scalability in your construction or trade business

"Running a construction business without having systems in place is like driving a car with no dashboard and your eyes closed. You can do it, but you're not going to last long. This book will open your eyes and give you the dashboard you need to operate a profitable construction business."
**—Shawn Van Dyke,** author of *Profit First for Contractors* and *The Paperwork Punch List*

"Chris Penasa and Small Business Growth Partners has helped hundreds of our members make their businesses stronger utilizing the principles outlined in this book. Too often owners don't take the full and necessary dive in assessing their companies. Whether you're looking to improve operations and profitability or simply looking to bring more sanity to your life in today's crazy home building and remodeling marketplace, *Drilling Down and Leveling Up* is a must-read for those in our industry. It will make you think differently about your company's future and help you uncover a better road map to achieve your goals as a business owner."
**—Bob Filka,** Chief Executive Officer, Home Builders Association of Michigan

"*Drilling Down and Leveling Up* reinforces the values that Small Business Growth Partners have been teaching our membership for years. This book will be a tremendous resource for any business owner in the trades."
**—Brad Boycks,** Executive Director, Wisconsin Builders Association

"*Drilling Down and Leveling Up* is a must-read for building contractors and trades businesses. You will learn real-world practical ways to improve your profitability and grow your company, rather than a bunch of theory and unproven ideas contained in many other business improvement books. By absorbing the information and putting it to work in your business, this book will definitely improve your business and your life."

**—Dr. Tony Alessandra,** author of *People Smart in Business* and *The Platinum Rule for DISC Sales Mastery*

*"Drilling Down and Leveling Up* should be mandatory reading for anyone who wants to thrive in our ever-changing business climate. I've personally witnessed profound cultural and financial changes in the business models of participating businesses in the Home Builders Association of Iowa."

**—Jay Iverson,** Executive Officer, Home Builders Association of Iowa

*"Drilling Down and Leveling Up* will help you get a closer look at your team, your processes, and your structure to help you work smarter, not harder, and increase profits. They understand the construction industry and have helped numerous builders. As an executive in an association that represents home builders, they have been a terrific partner to my members, and I highly recommend you learn from them."

**—Mike Means,** Executive Vice President, Oklahoma Home Builders Association

"This is a must-read book for anyone engaged as a small business owner in the residential construction industry. This book gives small-business owners the tools to be successful in an ever-changing market."

**—Rick Wajda,** Chief Executive Officer, Indiana Builders Association

*"Drilling Down and Leveling Up* is an insightful extension of the great work Chris and the SBGP team already provide to our members. If the feedback regarding the effectiveness of this book comes close to matching the feedback we regularly receive from our members already working with SBGP, its

concepts and tools for success will have a very long shelf life. Looking forward to implementing the book's principles with our HBA team."

**–Ted Leighty,** Chief Executive Officer, Colorado Association of Home Builders

"Small Business Growth Partners' coaching strategies work because the company's founders have experienced what it takes to thrive rather than merely survive while running a business. The systems they have developed are effective because they don't just provide suggestions and advice, they truly partner with their clients to help them improve and grow their companies. Rarely have I received so much positive feedback from a member program. *Drilling Down and Leveling Up* will serve as a helpful blueprint throughout the SBGP coaching process, as well as a great tool of reference as you lead your company successfully into the future."

**–M. Scott Norman, Jr.,** Executive Director, Texas Association of Builders

"*Drilling Down and Leveling Up* is the perfect title for what this book embodies. Every business looking to grow, achieve better profits, and attain success should utilize the tools discussed in this book. Many of our members who run small businesses are seeing success working with Chris Penasa to identifying strengths and weaknesses and taking their company to the next level."

**–M. Craig Toalson,** CAE, Chief Executive Officer, Home Builders Association of Virginia

"I never realized I was doing it all wrong until I met Chris Penasa. *Drilling Down and Leveling Up* will completely shift your paradigm on how to run a building company. He lays out step-by-step how to build your dream company with more profitability, easier sales, and freedom for the owner. His methodology changed my life, and it will change yours."

**–David Belman,** author of *Leadership Growth Hacks* and owner of Belman Homes

# DRILLING DOWN AND

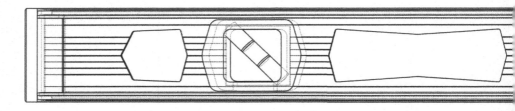

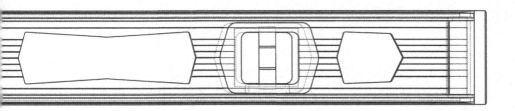

# LEVELING
# UP

Attaining consistency, profitability,
and scalability in your construction
or trade business

# CHRIS
# PENASA

# DEDICATION

I'd like to dedicate this book to all the Small Business Growth Partners clients who have trusted us to help them get control of their businesses, create fantastic teams, and build companies that are consistent, profitable, and a joy to run. Without our clients' dedication, entrepreneurial spirit, and good hearts, Growth Partners would not be able to make a difference in the lives of home builders, remodelers, and tradespeople around the country.

# TABLE OF CONTENTS

PREFACE        Our Story                                          1

INTRODUCTION                                                      7

BUSINESS HEALTH ASSESSMENT                                       15

CHAPTER 1     Change Starts with You                             23

CHAPTER 2     Strategy and Vision                                33

CHAPTER 3     The Profitability Puzzle                           45

CHAPTER 4     Leadership and Culture                             57

CHAPTER 5     Systemizing Your Business                          67

CHAPTER 6     Hiring and Onboarding                              79

CHAPTER 7     Managing Employees and Contractors                91

CHAPTER 8     Marketing                                         103

CHAPTER 9     Sales                                             117

CHAPTER 10    Taking Care of Customers                          131

CHAPTER 11    Leveling Up Your Financial Planning               141

CHAPTER 12    Painless Planning                                 153

CHAPTER 13    Continuous Improvement                            167

ACKNOWLEDGEMENTS                                                183

ABOUT SMALL BUSINESS GROWTH PARTNERS                            185

much they charge to build or remodel a home, leading many prospective home buyers and current homeowners to be suspicious of professionals in this field, believing that the contractors will take advantage of them if they let their guard down.

In reality, nothing could be further from the truth. Builders and trade company owners care about building and delivering a great product for their clients, and they try to offer fair prices to make a decent living. The trouble is how easy it is to run into problems along the way; projects become more complicated than anticipated, materials and labor cost more than expected, and it can take longer than anticipated to get a job done. Major long-term projects, such as building houses, only exacerbate the chances that things will go off track. With all of this in mind, I knew that if I wanted to make a real impact coaching small-business owners, then focusing on the construction and trade industries would be a perfect fit.

Our cofounder, Terry Elton, feels the same way. He grew up in industry, working at his father's excavating company from the time he was a child through college. After Terry graduated, his dad wanted him to take over the company, but Terry wanted to do other things. So his dad kept running the business on his own. He worked long hours and was always dedicated to serving his customers. Terry remembers fondly that his dad was truly excellent at his trade. But he was not a business guy. After 50 years, when he was ready to retire, all he could do was sell the equipment he no longer needed, pay the final bills, and turn off the lights. Despite owning a company for decades and dedicating his entire adult life to his craft, he didn't have a retirement fund or any significant savings. In fact, if he had worked for someone else all those years, he probably would have walked away with a lot more.

After watching his dad go through this experience, Terry had become hyper-aware of how many entrepreneurs think they have created a business, when in fact they really have just created a job for themselves. If the owner leaves the business, there's nothing left. At SBGP, Terry is passionate about helping other owners in the construction and trade industries shape their company such that their work doesn't consume every waking hour of their life while, at the same time, making enough to secure their future.

Terry and I wouldn't be where we are today without Carolyn Turner, our Chief Coaching Officer. Carolyn works directly with many of our clients and also leads our coaching practice. She came from a family business herself. After inventing an ingenious control mechanism to steer boats, her grandfather launched a company out of his basement in the 1950s, and his design quickly became the gold standard for steering ships, yachts, and other vessels. Carolyn was always interested in the company, but working there wasn't an option for her because her family felt strongly that women should not be involved in business.

From a young age, Carolyn loved the idea that business owners made things happen in the world. She recognized that the bigger a company becomes, the more impact it has. Her passion for growth led her to seek out corporate roles, where she built multimillion-dollar business lines from scratch within larger organizations. From there, she founded her own company, coaching leaders how to become more effective and improve their company from the top down.

Given that she had been excluded from joining her family business simply based on her gender, there is palpable irony in Carolyn's business acumen. Terry and I knew we needed her on our team. Luckily for us, Carolyn loves working with construction and trade businesses. She believes that <u>everyone needs a beautiful place to live</u>, and that the people who create those homes are truly gifted. She knows that a significant number of developers are great at building homes but struggle on the business side. After delivering a final product that's worth hundreds of thousands or even millions of dollars, many are exhausted and burned out, and take home profits that amount to mere pocket change. Being able to help those hardworking people improve their business lights her up every day.

Although my name is on the cover of this book as the author, Terry and Carolyn were right there with me every step of the way to make sure it would be as useful as it can possibly be for small-business owners, and especially construction and trade businesses. We are passionate about our line of work, and we can't wait to help you transform your business and bring more profits and joy into your life.

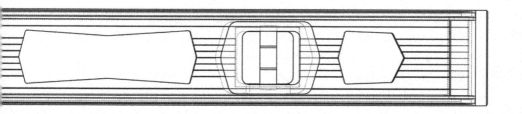

# INTRODUCTION

John Mohr started his home remodeling business in 2010, and he did beautiful work. He had an eye for detail, a knack for top-quality craftsmanship, and a passion for serving his customers. Although he had built a company that aligned with his expertise, he soon found that it wasn't enough to successfully scale his business.

John was two-thirds of the way over the cliff when we met him. He wasn't making nearly enough money to get by. In fact, he had an eyebrow-raising amount of debt. He couldn't personally handle every single job to make sure it was done right, and he was struggling to hire and retain reliable team members. Systems or processes for managing projects had never been established, which meant everyone did things in a different way, creating completely different levels of quality in the final product. Corners were cut on all kinds of jobs, which was becoming detrimental to the company's reputation. Bringing in new business became harder and harder, and John was finally at the end of his rope. He'd even decided that his best option would be to sell the company.

This is where John was when we first spoke with him. He'd

heard about Small Business Growth Partners through his home builders association and decided to give our coaching program a try as a last-ditch effort to save his company. My team and I meet owners who are in a variety of situations, but John was in a particularly bad spot. Virtually every aspect of his business needed an overhaul, and progress needed to be made quickly. But we saw so much potential in John. He was smart, talented, and dedicated; he just didn't have the knowledge he needed to make his business run smoother and successfully expand it. That's where my team and I came in.

We've worked with hundreds of small-business owners over the years who've shown the potential for greatness but are held back by their lack of knowledge in how to effectively scale a profitable company in the construction and trade industries. But we are also incredibly selective in who we choose to partner with. We only work with owners who are serious about their business and teams and are prepared to implement what they learn while working with us. Although John's situation was one of the messier ones we'd seen, we knew we could help him turn things around. We believed in him so much that we gave him a grant and covered part of his coaching fees so that cost wouldn't be a barrier for him.

Transformation didn't happen overnight, but John's business is in a totally different place today than it was a few years ago. He's making good money; he has a solid team in place; and he can rely on well-organized systems and processes across all aspects of the company. He no longer struggles with quality control in delivering a great product, and customers are spreading the word and supplying plenty of referrals.

Things have gone so well that John actually launched a second business doing millwork, which helps supply his remodeling company. Thanks to everything he learned from our coaching, he was able to easily create a new business that was successful from the start. In fact, his biggest remodeling competitor is now contracting with John to provide the millwork for them as well.

It's been a night-and-day turnaround. When we first started working with John, he was worried about his finances, his mental health, and his future. Today, he's in a totally different spot. He loves his job, and he's finding a new level of meaning in his work as he mentors his dedicated, hardworking employees.

We experience this kind of transformation with clients all the time at SBGP. Owners are frustrated that their business has stagnated—or things are going south and they can't seem to turn them around. They work crazy hours and struggle to pay their bills. Many of them don't enjoy going to work anymore, and their day-to-day reality doesn't align with their interests, strengths, or passions. To make matters worse, since business is stressful and unpleasant, it starts affecting their personal life. Outside of work, they are depressed and irritable, and can't enjoy the things that used to bring them happiness.

Personally, I know exactly what that feels like. It's almost as though your business has hijacked your life. It's such a hard spot to be in, especially when you have poured your heart and soul into a company. But the good news is that radical transformation is possible with some simple, targeted strategies that anyone can do when practiced on a consistent basis.

My team and I have developed a tested and proven system that helps construction and trade businesses take their organization to the next level. By partnering with owners to help them understand where things are breaking down and what to do about it, we're able to drive the kind of change John experienced in his home remodeling business. Instead of closing up shop, owners find themselves thriving. Not only are they profitable, they're happy. They have more free time, as well as the emotional energy to enjoy it. I can't even recall how many times I've heard a client say, "I feel like I have my life back!" That kind of statement never gets old. It's a reminder that SBGP is making a true difference for hardworking small-business owners.

Wanting to make a bigger impact is one reason my team and I decided to write this book. After seeing how far our clients go with coaching alone, we realized that we could accelerate their speed with a book that covers all of the most important principles in our coaching program.

If you've received this book from the SBGP team as a companion to coaching, we encourage you to read it before starting your own coaching program. Just like you would read a blueprint to understand where you're going with a project, this book is a guide for where you will go with coaching. Our programs are customized, and we always tailor our support to meet individual clients' needs, but it's helpful for you to know all the areas you can cover when it comes to enhancing your business.

# WHAT TO EXPECT IN THIS BOOK

Here's an overview of the topics you can expect in this book:

**Vision and Planning:** It's easy to get caught up in the day-to-day chaos of owning a business and feel like you don't have the bandwidth to be strategic and properly plan for the future. But just like when building a house, you need to understand the big picture to make sure you're on track to deliver. We'll help you identify where you want your business to go and create solid plans to get there.

**Marketing:** There are countless ways to market your business, but some strategies are much more effective than others for construction and trade businesses. Many owners waste time and money on initiatives that make little to no difference while overlooking crucial touchpoints with potential customers. Find out how to better prioritize and simplify your efforts for better results.

**Sales:** A crucial aspect of every company, sales can be elusive to master. When sales goals aren't met, it can be difficult to pinpoint where the process is breaking down. This is an area where we are especially excited to help, since almost every single one of our clients has been able to significantly improve their sales process and conversion rates with our support.

**Team:** Many construction and trade business owners got

their start by swinging a hammer, caulking tile, or project managing their jobs personally; they excelled at the work, so they formed a business around it. Most didn't launch their companies so that they could hire, train, manage, and motivate others. And yet, that's what a huge chunk of the job turns into when a company grows. Leading a team is an unavoidable part of being a successful business owner, and in this book, we'll help you take your skills to the next level.

**Processes and Systems:** When you're growing a business, you need to be able to step away from overseeing all the details of what's happening across the organization and trust that your team can handle it. Developing the right systems and processes will enable you to have rhythm and consistency in your business and free up a tremendous amount of your valuable time.

**Finances:** Whether you're good with numbers or not, you need to have a solid understanding of basic financial concepts and how to apply them in your business. Without doing this work, you might not realize that you're undercharging, or are set to run out of cash before clients pay you in full. We'll teach the key financial principles you need to know, such as calculating your breakevens, margins, and markups, and what happens if those numbers fluctuate. We will also share some simple and extremely valuable financial tracking templates and business "scorecards" that will give you a much better grasp of your key metrics, and how they are affecting your overall profitability—and sanity.

You might already recognize key areas in your business that need more attention. The self-assessment in the following section will help you identify internal opportunities and initiatives that could make a major and immediate impact. We strongly recommend that you read through all the chapters, even if you think you're already acing some of the topics. You could be surprised at how many opportunities you truly have to take your company to the next level.

Above all, don't get overwhelmed. Remember that success is built one step at a time. If you chunk down your goals and just keep putting one foot in front of the other, you will be amazed at how far you can go.

Below is a list of key terms that you should know.

**bit.ly link:** a URL link-shortening service used to redirect and share digital links

**cost of goods:** the amount paid for materials and labor used to build or remodel a home

**critical nonessentials:** things that lie outside the necessary or core part of a business (e.g., client birthday cards)

**customer relationship management (CRM) software:** a system generally used by companies for contact and database management

**DISC:** a behavioral self-assessment tool used to improve work productivity, teamwork, leadership, sales, and communication skills

**expenses (also known as overhead):** the costs of running a business, including rent, utilities, taxes, association fees, membership dues, office supplies, fuel, office staff, insurance, and marketing costs; are unrelated to project costs

**gross profit:** the difference between income and cost of goods

**gross profit margin (also known as gross profit percentage):** financial gain expressed as a percentage of income (gross profit/income); not always shown in Quickbooks, but can be easily calculated

**income:** money or revenue coming into a business

**key performance indicator (KPI):** quantifiable objective used to measure performance and the success of an employee, team, or organization

**lag indicator:** a financial sign of past performance

**lead funnel:** the qualification process a lead goes through in order to be deselected or passed to the sales team as a sales-qualified lead

**lead indicator:** a sign of performance that might predict future success

**lead magnet:** a marketing term for a free item or service that is given away for the purpose of gathering information on sales leads

**net ordinary income:** the amount of money left over after cost of goods and expenses have been paid (income minus cost of goods minus expenses)

**net profit margin (also known as net profit percentage):** net ordinary income expressed as a percentage of income (net ordinary income/income); not always shown in Quickbooks, but can be easily calculated

**one-liner:** a single sentence that clearly explains what a business offers and why people should buy from it

**one-sheeter:** a single page promotional document on a company

**professional services agreement (PSA):** a document used to create a contractually binding agreement between a business and customer

**sales process:** a predetermined, defined, and sequential series of steps to turn a qualified sales lead into a customer or client

**sales-qualified lead:** a potential customer or client within a target market that has the wherewithal to buy and is going to work with someone

**target market:** a particular group of customers or clients at whom a product or service is aimed

**unique selling proposition:** a trait that separates a business from its competition

**upward delegation:** when an employee brings a problem or issue to a more senior employee to solve

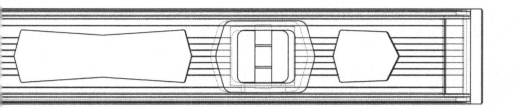

# BUSINESS HEALTH ASSESSMENT

*B*efore you move forward in the book, take a minute to do a short self-assessment of your business. This will help you set a baseline of where you are today. It will also enable you to identify what you should focus on next when it comes to evolving your business.

Respond to the following statements on a scale of one to five, with one being weak and five being strong.

## VISION AND PLANNING

1. **VISION**

   1 2 3 4 5
   ☐ ☑ ☐ ☐ ☐

   We have a clear vision that documents and communicates where the business is going, why that vision is important, and what the ultimate goal is.

---

2. **STRATEGIC BUSINESS PLAN**

   1 2 3 4 5
   ☐ ☑ ☐ ☐ ☐

   Our strategic business plan has been created and kept up to date.

---

### 3. ANNUAL AND QUARTERLY PLANNING SYSTEM

*1   2   3   4   5*
☐ ☐ 2 ☐ ☐

We have a planning system that consistently sets and prioritizes annual and quarterly goals and actions, enforces accountability, and tracks progress.

## MARKETING

### 1. TACTICAL MARKETING PLAN

*1   2   3   4   5*
☐ ☐ ☐ ☐ ☐

We have a plan for how to produce a steady, predictable, and sustainable number of sales leads and a positive return on marketing investments.

### 2. UNIQUE SELLING PROPOSITION (USP) AND GUARANTEE

*1   2   3   4   5*
☐ ☐ ☐ ☐ ☐

We use these to attract ideal clients who are willing to pay a higher price for quality service and superior craftsmanship.

### 3. REFERRALS

*1   2   3   4   5*
☐ ☐ ☐ ☐ ☐

We have a process to gather referrals from clients, trade partners, and other business relationships to provide the majority of sales leads. We also receive a constant flow of five-star reviews.

## SALES

### 1. SALES PROCESS

*1   2   3   4   5*
☐ ☐ ☐ ☐ ☐

We have created and continue to refine a carefully

organized sales process and use it consistently within all sales activities. We make sure customers/clients know why we work the way we do. We—rather than our clients—drive our sales process.

2. **SALES GOALS AND METRICS**

*1  2  3  4  5*
☐ ☐ ☐ ☐ ☐

We consistently track sales progress and key metrics, such as conversion rate. We identify sales goals and hold our team accountable to them.

3. **CUSTOMER RELATIONSHIP MANAGEMENT (CRM) SYSTEM**

*1  2  3  4  5*
☐ ☐ ☐ ☐ ☐

We have fully implemented a CRM software solution that captures leads and tracks sales progress and results.

# TEAM

1. **LEADERSHIP AND MANAGEMENT SKILLS**

*1  2  3  4  5*
☐ ☐ ☐ ☐ ☐

We consistently develop our own leadership and management skills and develop the next generation of leaders and managers for the business.

2. **ROLES AND RESPONSIBILITIES**

*1  2  3  4  5*
☐ ☐ ☐ ☐ ☐

All roles and responsibilities are written down and communicated to team members.

### 3. HIRING PROCESS

*1 2 3 4 5*
☐ ☐ ☐ ☐ ☐

We have a defined hiring process, and our recruiting pipeline always has more than enough qualified candidates for open positions. Requirements are identified early and included in strategic and quarterly planning.

---

## PROCESSES AND SYSTEMS

### 1. KEY BUSINESS PROCESSES PLAN

*1 2 3 4 5*
☐ ☐ ☐ ☐ ☐

We have identified our key business processes and have a plan to define and continually refine them and improve the handoffs between functions of the business (e.g., marketing to sales, sales to design, design to operations, operations to warranty).

---

### 2. KEY PERFORMANCE INDICATORS (KPI)

*1 2 3 4 5*
☐ ☐ ☐ ☐ ☐

We have a KPI system that clearly identifies the most important business success indicators, which we consistently measure and manage.

---

### 3. CONTINUOUS PROCESS IMPROVEMENT

*1 2 3 4 5*
☐ ☐ ☐ ☐ ☐

We have a system to manage our ongoing efforts to improve our services and processes. These efforts create incremental improvements over time, or sometimes breakthrough improvements all at once.

---

# OPERATIONS

1. **PROJECT MANAGEMENT SYSTEM**  1 2 3 4 5 □ □ □ □ □
   We have a system to track all active projects, including scheduling and communication.

2. **CHANGE ORDER PROCESS**  1 2 3 4 5 □ □ □ □ □
   We have a defined change order process that is followed consistently.

3. **COMMUNICATION PROCESS**  1 2 3 4 5 □ □ □ □ □
   We communicate with our clients/customers/trade partners on their projects in a clear way and on a timely basis.

# FINANCIAL

1. **BREAK EVEN**  1 2 3 4 5 □ □ □ □ □
   We know what our revenue needs to support the business, including payroll and overhead expenses.

2. **NET PROFIT MARGIN**  1 2 3 4 5 □ □ □ □ □
   We have a set net profit goal and are managing to that goal.

### 3. PRICING AND MARGIN AUDITS (JOB COSTING)

*1  2  3  4  5*
☐ ☐ ☐ ☐ ☐

Actual project results are compared with expected project results, and adjustments are made to pricing and processes as necessary.

## ACCOUNTABILITY

*1  2  3  4  5*
☐ ☐ ☐ ☐ ☐

### 1. ACCOUNTABILITY SYSTEM

Every team member understands what they are responsible for and is accountable to the team for delivering results.

*1  2  3  4  5*
☐ ☐ ☐ ☐ ☐

### 2. SCORECARDS

We use visual scorecards that clearly show the health of the business at a glance. Every team member has at least one personal metric that represents their individual contributions to the business.

*1  2  3  4  5*
☐ ☐ ☐ ☐ ☐

### 3. MANAGEMENT DECISIONS

Responsibilities and the authority to make decisions are delegated to the lowest possible level in the company.

Total: _____

After filling out the assessment, identify the three items that are most important for you to work on for your business:

1. _____

2. _____

3. _____

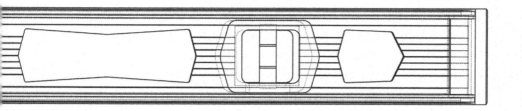

## CHAPTER 1

## CHANGE STARTS WITH YOU

Making a good living running a small business is no small feat—especially in the home building and trade industries. It's amazing that no matter how much you work, there is always a seemingly endless list of things to do. Even if you have the best intentions for being strategic about your business, it's hard to carve out time to sit down, fix what isn't working, and figure out how to take your company to the next level.

As business coaches, we love helping builders because so many of them don't realize that improving their business is a lot easier than they might imagine. We know firsthand that the individuals we coach are good, honest, hardworking people. They care about helping their employees and their families. They want to do a great job to help their clients live their fairy-tale "happily ever after" in the home of their dreams. However, they can't always see the simple things they could do differently to drive greater success in their organization.

Change can be a tricky subject because a lot of people have been conditioned to believe that if they need to change something, it is only because they are doing it *wrong*. That's not how we look at it. Change isn't about being right or wrong; it's about being empowered to do things *better* than before. Chances are, your 20th project went a lot smoother than your first one did. This is true for learning just about anything in life, from bowling to driving a car to learning how to use your new grill. The first time you do something, you're likely to stumble through it. It's a little uncomfortable, but it gets better from there. Most of the people we coach are first-time business owners who have never experienced significant growth or scaled a business before. It only makes sense that they would have some room for improvement.

*You're reading this book because you want different results than what you're currently getting.* The fact that you are taking the time to learn the concepts that could help transform your business means that you believe in yourself and your talent as an owner. If you didn't, you wouldn't have ever picked up this book. One crucial point to understand before you dive into the knowledge and exercises in later chapters is that *change starts with you.* As the title of this chapter points out, no one else in your business will care as much as you do about your success, or be willing to work as hard as you to make it happen. This simple truth is the number-one piece of wisdom we want you to absorb because it empowers you to take the reins in your business and assume the responsibility for your company's future.

To get better results, you have to start doing things differently. But first, you have to *think* differently.

A lot of clients come to SBGP worried that their business is beyond the point where it can be saved. They don't know if they have what it takes to turn things around, and they aren't shy about sharing their hesitations with us. We empathize with our clients and understand how difficult it is to scale a business. But, as we like to say, people can either make excuses or they can make it happen, but they can't do both.

If you just started working with a coach, or you're about to embark on your coaching journey, chances are you're in a tough spot. By now, you've probably already done all of the easy work that you know how to do. The only things that are left are the projects and tasks that seem difficult, confusing, or totally foreign. You will have to face what you've been avoiding, and a coach can help guide you. Instead of walking an unknown path alone, you'll have an industry expert walk with you and guide you along the way. Coaches offer encouragement, support, and sage insight that can make a world of difference in how you run your business. Even if you've never been able to accomplish successful change in your company, now is the time you'll experience real transformation. That's why you need to adopt a mindset of belief and a glimmer of hope that maybe—just maybe—you can do this.

Many of our new clients throw their hands up and say something like this: "I'm kind of buying what you're telling me, and I'm not sure it will work, but I am willing to give it a try." That willingness is when the light bulb turns on. Once you believe in yourself, everything in your business has the chance to improve. It's that simple.

## MASTER RHYTHM AND CONSISTENCY

Two themes are paramount to your success as a business owner: getting into the right rhythm and doing things with consistency. You've probably experienced what this feels like during periods when everything in your business just seemed to flow. Money was coming in, clients were happy, and all of your employees were busy making an impact. The link between rhythm and results isn't pseudoscience; everything in life has a cadence. From the rising and setting of the sun to the gravitational pull of the moon on the oceans' tides, there is a rhythm that orchestrates everything in nature. As a byproduct of their natural instincts, humans also subconsciously fall into this type of organized structure. In this book, you will learn to become more intentional about your rhythm, both personally and in your business.

The famous philosopher Aristotle once said, "We are what we repeatedly do. Excellence then is not an act, but a habit."

Getting into a successful rhythm is about developing smart habits that serve you well. What you do consistently determines your outcome in life. To achieve excellence in your business, you can't go about each day randomly without a plan. Along the same lines, it doesn't work to do the right thing once and forget about it. You have to get into a rhythm of consistently doing the work that matters most.

In the beginning, this can be uncomfortable, since you won't have a solid grasp on how to execute all of the actions that are supposed to become your new habits. To make it easier to understand, we like to break this complex process down using what's known as the Four Stages of Learning to walk our clients through the act of turning a new action into an engrained habit. The process was developed in the 1970s by Noel Burch of Gordon Training International.

## THE FOUR STAGES OF LEARNING

Every time you attempt to do something new, there is a learning curve. Most people believe that building knowledge and skills just takes practice, but it's a little more nuanced than that. Whether you are a rookie business owner or a seasoned veteran, you will rotate through Four Stages of Learning each time. It is an ongoing journey that you repeat over and over as you add new skills to your toolbelt.

### Stage 1: Unconscious Incompetence
In this first stage, *you don't know what you don't know.* Instead of having a skill, you have a blind spot. In business, it's easy to exist in this stage for a long time. It isn't a particularly uncomfortable spot to be in, since ignorance is bliss, or so they say. However, sticking around in Stage 1 means that you'll miss out on all kinds of growth opportunities. To move on to the next stage, you must first establish a curiosity and drive to learn more.

### Stage 2: Conscious Incompetence
In Stage 2, you become aware of your lack of knowledge in a

certain area and see the gap between where you are and where you could be. For example, you experience an impressive sales process at another business and realize how much your own company could improve in that regard. But you aren't sure how to get there. Since most people don't enjoy the feeling of being incompetent, this stage can be uncomfortable, or even downright painful. However, once you know your weaknesses, you can get to work on building new competencies.

### Stage 3: Conscious Competence

In Stage 3, you learn how to do something new, but it still takes a fair amount of mental work to complete the task. For example, you learn how to properly onboard your new employees, but you still need to closely follow a checklist and reference your notes for each step of the process. Stage 3 takes a lot of energy to consciously think about every action you need to take, but the good news is that it only becomes easier from there. Once actions become habits, you'll be able to move much faster because you'll no longer need to think about them.

### Stage 4: Unconscious Competence

By the time you reach Stage 4, you've become fully proficient at a new skill or task. In fact, you've gotten so good that you don't even have to think about it anymore; you could practically do it with your eyes closed. Chances are you already feel like this when you're in the field doing something you have done a million times. The goal is to start feeling this unconscious competence for the vast majority of functions in your business.

To make serious changes at your organization, you'll need to get comfortable with the realization that you don't know everything. You can master anything you put your mind to, but it takes hard work and determination to have a continuous learning mindset. Any time you learn a new skill, you will rotate through these Four Stages of Learning. This is important to keep in mind, because just like the natural rhythm of the four seasons, these Four Stages are ongoing. Making this mindset shift will help you not only stay humble, but create the rhythm and consistency needed to effectively scale a success-ful business.

# LEARN TIME MANAGEMENT

When owners no longer have a boss managing them, they are free to do whatever they want. But the question we ask our clients is, *"Are you doing what you should be doing?"*

Think back to the last time you were an employee. Did you hold yourself as accountable as your former boss did, or did you let yourself cut a few corners here and there? If you could have that same level of discipline in your business as you did when you reported to a boss, imagine what you could accomplish in a year.

To level up your accountability, we recommend that you treat yourself like your most important customer and make it a priority to invest time to work on your business. With our coaching clients, we've found that all it takes is just two to three hours per week to make a real difference. But you will need to actually schedule this time in your calendar to make sure it gets done. If something comes up, don't just skip your designated time to work on your business. Instead, treat it like you're meeting with your most important customer and reschedule ASAP. This takes a lot of discipline, but it also builds rhythm and consistency, which is how you keep your business running smoothly.

## URGENT VERSUS IMPORTANT QUADRANTS

One helpful tool that we encourage our clients to use to find more time in their schedule is called the Eisenhower Matrix, commonly known as the Urgent-Important Matrix. Each time a new task comes in, you can quickly rank it using this system to determine whether it is a good use of your time. This is to make sure that you don't get caught in the "urgency trap," where you waste valuable time focusing on the wrong things.

### Important and Urgent
When a task is both important and urgent, you need to get it

done right away, so you should always do it before taking care of your other responsibilities. You have no other choice but to prioritize this kind of task—whether or not it's something you feel like working on at this particular moment. Sometimes, urgency is ramped up on a project because it was ignored until the last minute due to procrastination. Other times, something critical pops up out of the blue and needs to be handled immediately. Either way, if a task falls into this category, do it as soon as possible. This is also known as "firefighting," as it is stressful and disruptive. For these tasks, your focus should be on how they ended up being important and urgent in the first place. As more base systems and processes take hold in your business, time spent in this area will become less and less.

### Important but Not Urgent

When something is important but not urgent, you need to schedule a time to do it in the near future. This is the zone where you focus on planning, thinking ahead, and putting systems and processes in place. These types of activities are essential to running your business efficiently, even though they don't need to be done right now. The trick is not putting these responsibilities off so long that they eventually become urgent and you have to drop everything to handle them. Instead, schedule a time on your calendar to knock these things out without procrastinating.

### Not Important but Urgent

If something isn't important but needs to be done urgently, you need to delegate it to someone else. You could have a direct report take the lead, or you could outsource it to someone outside the company. In either case, you want to make sure the task gets completed in a timely manner so you don't have to worry about it. Tasks like these can often be a great fit for an assistant. When someone knows you well, they can answer questions on your behalf so that trivial interruptions don't throw you off track.

## Not Important and Not Urgent

These activities are great examples of things you should say "no" to. Whether you delegate them to someone else or just say that you don't have time, these tasks should be avoided at all costs because they won't help your bottom line.

|  | URGENT | NOT URGENT |
|---|---|---|
| **IMPORTANT** | **Firefighting**<br>• Material not on site<br>• Upset customers<br>• Subs don't show<br>• Site safety issues | **Quality Zone**<br>• Strategic planning<br>• Relationship building<br>• Management by walking around<br>• Recognizing new opportunities<br>• Consistent post-project reconciliations |
| **NOT IMPORTANT** | **Distraction**<br>• Upward delegation<br>• Some emails and meetings<br>• Gravitation to field work (when you have a project manager)<br>• Payroll and bookkeeping | **Time Wasting**<br>• Marketing to wrong customers<br>• Trivial, busy work<br>• Trying to turn not-good-fit clients into raving fans |

As you begin implementing changes to improve your business, you might feel a bit overwhelmed. We use the Urgency Matrix to help business owners regain a sense of control over their schedule to minimize this overwhelming feeling. In fact, the previous graphic is taken from an actual client coaching session where we helped the owner understand how to incorporate the four quadrants into his unique business blueprint. When he was able to focus on what mattered most, he found himself with even more time in his schedule. Having a new level of effectiveness enabled him to spark the transformation he was looking for in his company. Today, this business owner's company is thriving.

Every business has areas that need improvement, but your ability to make changes comes down to how efficiently you can use your time. The better equipped you are at focusing only on actions that make an impact, the more effective you will be as a leader. This change, while slight, has the power to make a profound shift in your day-to-day reality, as well as in your business's trajectory.

## WHEN YOU CHANGE, SO WILL YOUR BUSINESS

If the prospect of making changes still feels a little overwhelming, remember that you don't have to make all of the tough decisions on your own anymore. Working with a seasoned coach who has assisted many other contractors in a similar position as the one you are in now can feel like a lifesaver. Having a trusted advisor who is on your side and wants you to succeed can take away some of the fear and anxiety that comes with making any adjustments to the business that puts food on your table. Change may be uncomfortable, but we want you to remember that making changes means making progress.

Sure, along the way you may experience some growing pains, but as you read through the lessons in this book and apply the same practical advice we've used to coach hundreds of builders and trade company owners who have been in your shoes, you'll start to develop a newfound confidence in yourself. This is the spark that can ignite real transformation, not only in your business but in your personal life as well. We've met business owners who were stressed out, underpaid, and bitter about spending long hours away from their family. We've worked with them to make simple changes that made them feel like they got their life back. This is the promise we have in store for you, and we will be there helping you every step of the way to make it a reality.

We can't do it for you, and just like building a house one nail a time, it won't magically happen overnight. But when you begin to change, so will your business. Your employees and customers—and even you—will be amazed at how different your business and life can look if you commit to taking the first step toward changing.

Remember, without this challenging self-work and the change that it brings, you would never have the type of growth you've dreamt of having for your business. This is what we've had to help many of our clients realize, and it is the biggest lesson in understanding that *change starts with you*. It might be the most challenging aspect of the journey, but it is also the most pivotal in helping you create the business you've always wanted.

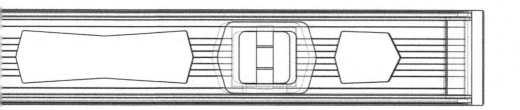

# CHAPTER 2

## STRATEGY AND VISION

When you first start your business, the thrill of getting paying clients is one of the best feelings in the world. Having enough work to pay the bills can be a real challenge, so you take on whatever comes your way. Even if you find yourself working on an unusual mix of projects, it can still be a freeing experience to know that you are capable of making money working for yourself.

This is a familiar story that a lot of entrepreneurs and business owners can relate to when they first start out. Unfortunately, many people continue on this path for months, years, or even decades. Instead of being strategic about what they want to work on or whom they want to work with, they just keep reacting to the business that comes in. They keep their head down and work hard, but almost all of their energy goes toward managing current projects. When they finally come up for air, their business often looks completely different than they had originally imagined.

Maybe this has happened to you at some point in your journey. Perhaps you pictured working with a certain kind of client, but those aren't the people who are reaching out to you.

Or you dreamt of working on a particular type of project, but in reality you rarely sell that kind of work (e.g., lake homes). When you have a reactive approach to your business growth and development, you let other people shape your company. Without following a vision, you'll end up somewhere—but who knows where that will be.

Building a business is just like building a house. You wouldn't start without a blueprint and just see where the hammer and nails take you. It's critical to have a plan and know what the end game is. That's how you know when you're making the right decisions. That's also how you inspire both employees and customers to want to work with you.

In this chapter, we'll focus on business strategy fundamentals. Whether your company has been around for decades or is brand new, go back to basics and make sure you're headed in the right direction.

Our clients sometimes forget that they have the power to shape their business into whatever they want it to be. We love getting business owners to a point where they feel excited and inspired to become more strategic, but it can also be a little intimidating for them. (With so many options, how do they determine what's right?)

Our best advice is to be honest with yourself about where you want your company—and your personal life—to go in the future. What will success really look like in 5, 10, or 25 years? When you know the outcome you want to create, it's just a back-engineering process to develop timelines and goals. Pair that with a commitment to follow your vision, and you can trust that you're on the right path.

## THREE STEPS TO FINDING YOUR NICHE

It's hard to say "no" to eager potential customers who offer you money. But taking on anything that comes along is a sure-fire way to create a lot of problems for your company—and for yourself on a personal level.

So many owners are afraid to become more selective about

the kind of work they do. They are worried about their bottom line because they've been conditioned to believe that they have to increase their revenue no matter the type of work that comes their way. However, sometimes saying "yes" to everything actually hurts profitability. What business owners don't realize is that niching down—in other words, focusing on a specific niche—is one of the best ways to earn even more in the long run. A niche gives you a leg up on your competitors because it allows you to articulate your value, which helps your business stand out.

Niching down can help you find more financial success, and it can also help you find work that you truly enjoy. Sometimes, in the early stages of a business, you aren't able to be strategic about whom you want to work with or have enough experience to really hone in on your favorite types of projects. But if you begin to take on a lot of work that you discover you don't particularly enjoy, you can experience burnout, exhaustion, and mounting stress levels that kill the passion and drive that led you to start your business in the first place. That's why it's so important to constantly be aware of the choices you make and the actions you take, and understand how they affect your business's trajectory.

Choosing your niche is tough. As you think about all of the possibilities and directions your business could go, you'll realize that you have more talents and skills than any single company should have as service offerings. Every business owner faces this dilemma, but it's especially true for builders because they can build anything. It doesn't matter if a prospect needs a kitchen remodeled or an entirely new summer lake house built—your team can probably do both projects well. In fact, we'd bet there are dozens of things you *could* help people with, but that there are probably only a handful of viable products or service you really *want* to offer your customers. The hard work lies in deciding what to specialize in and following through with that plan. As the old adage says, you don't want to be a jack of all trades but master of none.

To make this process easy, we like to challenge our clients to think of their niche as an intersection where three important factors all line up and come together to serve their customers.

### 1. First, ask yourself, "What do I love to do?"

Figuring out where you can make money off of your passions is the first step to running a business that you love and enjoy. If you aren't passionate about it, it's tough to justify putting in long hours at the office, no matter how much money you are making.

A classic example of this is the dichotomy between builders who love working one-on-one with clients on custom builds versus builders who prefer to work on spec builds. Each of these specialties has different pros and cons associated with them, but whether they are the right fit for your business depends on what you enjoy. Some builders like to focus on spec homes, and they pony up the cash to fund the development themselves, which means they take on the financial risk. This is a great project for builders who don't want to spend a lot of time dealing with people during the building process and have time to commit to a vision in hopes of a big payout in the future. But on the flip side, other builders don't have any interest in doing this kind of work. They might want to take on custom homes because they love interacting with people and coming up with creative solutions for their unique needs. These projects require a lot of face time with clients, which can present its own challenges, but also plenty of opportunities to get referrals and repeat business. We can't tell you what you're passionate about, but we can encourage you to find out through consistent trial and error. Know that it's OK to not enjoy everything. The sooner you can be honest with yourself about what you like and don't like, the sooner you'll be able to find your stride.

### 2. Next, ask yourself, "What does the market want?"

You may love modern architecture, but if you live in a city like Richmond, Virginia, you could be stuck doing remodels on older colonial houses. Remember, markets fluctuate depending on geographic area, so you need to find out what types of opportunities are available for your specific location.

One of the easiest ways to find the sweet spot in your market is to identify how you currently generate most of your revenue. While it won't always be your niche per se, most of the time it's a good indication of the intersection between the market's demand and your ability to fulfill this need.

### 3. Finally, ask yourself, "What do I already have experience in?"

One way to think about experience is to consider the types of clients you work with. You can do this by niching down on demographics. Many small businesses find that they work with the same types of people over and over, even when the services they provide vary.

For example, some of our clients build a lot of homes for families with kids. Others tend to focus on building for empty nesters. Some of our clients have even found that they had phenomenal experiences helping families who needed handicap-accessible homes. Many of these businesses did one project well and it helped them bring in work with a new client from a similar background. Maybe it was from referrals, or from having experience in that type of project in their portfolio.

On the flip side, sometimes our clients work with customers who are unlike anyone they've worked with before. This can be a quick way to realize that there are promising new opportunities on the horizon, or a learning experience to avoid certain prospects in the future. In either case, experience makes a difference when it comes to analyzing your niche and becoming more proactive about shaping it.

Successful business owners often tell us that their niche was right in front of their nose the whole time, but it took them *years* to figure it out. This often occurs when companies are really good at doing one particular kind of project. Since it comes easily to them—almost second nature, in fact—they usually take that type of work for granted.

When something is easy for your team to pull off, it's a good indication that that type of work is a strong contender for being your company's niche—assuming you enjoy the work. Sometimes, the best solution is the simplest solution, and finding your niche means doubling down on what you already do well.

# HOW TO FIND YOUR IDEAL CLIENT

Being intentional about which customers you serve is important because when you love the people you serve, you love the work that you do. A lot of business owners think that ideal clients come in all shapes and sizes, but you want to get more specific than that when mapping out your perfect client. Unlike narrowing down your favorite ice cream cone out of Baskin-Robbins' 31 original flavors—which may take some research-intensive time—ideal clients usually fall into similar predictable traits (such as location, age, life stage, etc.) that help you identify them more easily. To help tease this out, we like to use an Ideal Client Profile tool. If you look at the template, you can see that this doesn't need to be super complex.

First, you'll want to identify the geographic range for where your ideal client lives, which will help eliminate clients who are too far away. Next, you can add more-specific descriptors, such as age, socioeconomic status, life stage, occupation, interests, and personality traits. It's important to brainstorm what types of people you like working with; until you write it down, you may not be aware you even have any preferences.

Once you've filled in a general profile of the ideal client, write down what such a client values when working with a builder or trade company. Different types of people value very different things, so make sure you're thinking this through and coming up with answers that truly align with your ideal client (e.g., not everyone cares about saving money).

Next, draft one or two sentences that describe your ideal client based on the information you just wrote down. Some of the business owners we work with are amazed at the clarity this exercise provides because they are finally able to articulate their target market.

| Ideal Client Profile | Where are they? | 45-minute radius of office; tri-county area of Main, Washington; and Summit County. |
| --- | --- | --- |
| | Who are they? | Second-time move-up buyers, married with dual incomes, budget-conscious with professional careers. Or, boomers, married and downsizing, have professional careers, and often can pay cash, snowbirds. |
| | What do they value? | Don't want condo/assisted living yet. Willing to pay for what they want/higher quality/choice--but not to be overwhelmed by 100 percent fully custom. They value a simplified process with a starting point. |
| | Our Ideal Clients... | Prefer to live in smaller communities near Summit County. They are single professionals, married couples with dual incomes, or empty nesters with a solid net worth who value family, quality, and reputation. They want a simple, proven process with some flexibility as well. |

# HOW TO CREATE A COMPANY ONE-LINER AND DIFFERENTIATE YOUR UNIQUE SELLING PROPOSITION

The next piece of the ideal-client puzzle is to create your company one-liner and identify your unique selling proposition. This aspect of your niche ties back to your vision for where you want your company to go. The one-liner is essentially an elevator pitch for your business, and it can take some work to craft the right words to clearly articulate your value and positioning in the market. To make this easier, we've broken the process down into three parts that you need to identify when writing your one-liner:

- ❖ **The Problem** – What is the main pain point you intend to solve for customers?
- ❖ **The Product** – What is the detailed product or service you offer that solves the problem?
- ❖ **The Result** – What is the positive outcome your customer will experience if they buy your product or service?

Once you've brainstormed each of these and written down your pain-problem-solution answers, you will use this information to create a compelling one-sentence summary, otherwise known as your company one-liner.

This exercise can be enlightening—even if you've been in business for many years. Having a clearly defined one-liner helps drive your vision for the future and factors into every action you and your employees take, so don't skip this work.

Finally, you will need to use the insights you receive from doing this exercise to list your differentiators and unique selling proposition. This is where you separate yourself from the rest of your competition. If you've correctly identified your pain-problem-solution format, this last step will be pretty easy—just compare your solution to what your competitors offer.

See the following example for inspiration, and download a blank version of this template from our website: drilldownlevelup.com/resources. If you are confused about this last step (or any of the definitions in this exercise), we encourage you to ask for help from your dedicated SBGP coach.

| | |
|---|---|
| **The Problem** | *They don't have a lot or can't find the ideal spot (lot availability in desirable locations). Buyers are often frustrated by lack of or poor communication and disorganized process. Some simply don't know where to start. They have a fear or stigma that everything is over budget.* |
| **The Product** | *Strong relationships with vendors, transparent and proactive communication (empathetic) that is organized, obsessed with details, responsiveness.* |
| **The Result** | *Comfort knowing they made a great move.* |
| **Pull It All Together** | *Building a custom home can feel overwhelming with decisions, budgets, and timing. ABC Home Builder provides expert guidance and manages the details to help minimize the stress and fulfill your dream.* |
| **1** | *Schedule integrity by doing it right the first time with thoughtful design and thorough preparation.* |
| **2** | *Solid relationships with trades.* |
| **3** | *Caring approach; we build like we're building for family, and we make it easy.* |

# HOW TO NARROW DOWN YOUR SERVICE OFFERINGS

Now that you've discovered the intersection where your passion meets a profitable niche, identified your ideal clients, and articulated your unique value, it's time to revisit your service offerings. Unless you run a lemonade stand, your company likely has a mix of services for different purposes.

Some projects (such as building custom homes) are big and generate a lot of income. They are great because you don't have to sell many of them, and they keep you busy for a long time. But if things are slow and the economy is bad, selling only this kind of product can make it harder to stay profitable. Smaller projects (such as remodeling jobs) can be a great source of consistent income, and can keep your employees and subs busy. That's one reason so many companies do both types of work (although we personally don't think that's an ideal strategy in the long term).

When you take these factors into account, you must also consider how your service offerings can be custom tailored to strategically grow your ideal customer base. For instance, maybe you don't like doing small bathroom remodels, despite such jobs being great low-ticket projects that could help you get easy foot-in-the-door sales with new clients. Taking them on won't make you as much money as full home remodels do, but they could funnel new clients into your business and make it much easier to sell them your big, expensive services, having proven yourself as a reputable company that can handle such smaller jobs.

As you fine-tune and figure out which services you want to offer, you can continually refine your business model to fit your ideal client profile. While we recommend keeping things simple by focusing on what you enjoy, we also recognize that there's an element of strategy here. You might need to continue offering additional services outside your ideal niche to keep the lights on—at least temporarily. Talk with an SBGP coach about how to phase out products and services that aren't in your niche, while maintaining good profitability overall.

## AVOID SHINY-OBJECT SYNDROME

One of the biggest obstacles to niching down your business is succumbing to the seductive snares of shiny-object syndrome. Let's pretend you get a new lead on a client or project that looks exciting—or "shiny." It may be attractive because it seems like a new direction for your business, or maybe you hope it will provide a quick cash windfall. However, once you start working on the project, you discover that it eats up a lot of time and energy and is actually a distraction or time suck that keeps you from doing the work you need to carry out your business plan. You've just been snared by the shiny-object syndrome.

Small-business owners are notorious for chasing shiny new opportunities that look good in the short term but don't pan out in the long run. Sometimes it's necessary to take calculated risks, but a lot of times people chase after ideas that push the business in different directions without thinking them through. This can lead to unintended consequences, and time-consuming headaches putting out fires down the road.

Part of being selective about the services you want to offer your customer base is recognizing that shiny-object projects aren't about what's best for the future of your company; rather, they are about instant gratification. Long term, they can actually be detrimental in taking you away from bigger, higher-paying projects you really enjoy. It's easy to get distracted, and before you know it, you've built a business around the customers who call you, instead of the ones you want to intentionally go after. As the owner, it's vital that you steer clear of time-wasting activities and only focus on work that aligns with your niche and vision. Remember, the more time you spend chasing down the "shiny" projects, the less time you have to improve your skills and master your bread-and-butter projects. In the early years of Small Business Growth Partners, we were tempted (and even encouraged by some) to look at other industries besides construction and trade companies, but we stuck with our long-term vision and didn't waiver. This one decision made a huge impact on what SBGP is today.

## STAY FOCUSED ON YOUR VISION

Every small-business owner starts with a vision, and it almost always evolves over time. Whether you've had your business for years or recently launched a new venture, we encourage you to focus on the topics in this chapter and give them the thought and consideration they deserve. You might find that your company has gone in a different direction than you originally anticipated. Maybe that's a good thing, but maybe you need to redirect.

Vision is important because it enables you to put in the extra elbow grease to handle the day-to-day tasks that tend to pile up on your plate. We like to think of vision as an owner's biggest mindset tool. Nothing will motivate you as much as the pursuit of your vision.

As you drill down and get more strategic about your business's blueprint, it's important that you hone in on your niche intersection. Find projects you enjoy that meet the needs of your market and give you confidence and experience. These are the key qualifications for creating a business that can grow and thrive in the long term. Of course, as you grow your business, you'll find that there's a lot more to it than that. But these are the foundational elements that can set you on the right track for building a business that is fun and enjoyable to run.

Finally, we like to inform our clients that having a plan and taking action on that plan are two very different things. Starting with a vision is important, but incorporating that vision into your actions is what gives you a foothold in the market. To put it simply, how effective you are at achieving your vision comes down to how successfully you can niche down and follow through. If you're intentional and strategic about these things, you will be able to level up your business in no time.

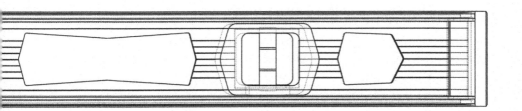

# CHAPTER 3

## THE PROFITABILITY PUZZLE

Imagine being at an NFL game and watching your favorite team go up against its greatest rival. (I'm picturing the Green Bay Packers versus the Chicago Bears.) The Packers' star running back makes a break through the Bears' defense and sprints across the goal line for an uncontested touchdown. Everyone around you in the stands cheers and high-fives their neighbors, but the celebrations are cut short when mysteriously, the points aren't added to the scoreboard. People are confused, asking around to find out what's going on. Was there a penalty flag on the play? Is there a problem with the scoreboard? You see a referee step forward and address the press booth to make an announcement. A hush washes over the stunned onlookers in the crowd. "We've decided not to keep score for today's game," the referee announces sheepishly. "The numbers look a bit complicated. Instead of adding up the score, we're just going to keep playing without it."

If your hometown is anything like mine, this scenario might cause mass pandemonium. Think about how absurd that would be. Players, fans, and coaches on both sides simply wouldn't stand for it. How long do you think it would take before the fans would empty the bleachers and mayhem would erupt in the parking lot? This isn't a backyard BBQ; it's a professional football game. Fans rooting for both teams would ask, "What's the point of playing if you aren't going to keep score?"

The same philosophy is true for your business. Without realizing it, many entrepreneurs fall into this same type of absurdity. If you don't know your numbers or understand basic financial concepts such as margin and markup, it's like playing a game without keeping score. You have no reference point to know what winning even looks like.

In this context, not keeping score sounds crazy. But you probably know how easy it is to get into a situation where you don't know the numbers for your business. As entrepreneurs, some of our core values are grit and perseverance. We know things won't always be perfect, and we have to weather the storms and keep pushing to make things better. This kind of entrepreneurial mindset can serve us very well in some ways but be an Achilles' heel in others.

When it comes to being profitable, numbers matter. Keeping your head down and continuing to work your butt off year after year may not get you the results you want. Instead of just working harder, you need to also work smarter. And one of the core things to focus on is knowing your numbers so that you can make the right decisions for your business. For example, adjusting your pricing by just 1 to 2 percent can turn into thousands of dollars more in profit at the end of each year. This alone can be the tipping point to turn your business profitable and put more money into your own pocket. But if you don't know how to tweak your numbers to get the results you want, you're operating on luck rather than on proven strategy.

When we coach builders and trade company owners, we find a lot of people stuck in a similar position. They deliver a great product to their customers. They take care of their employees and pay their bills. Then, they keep for themselves what little money is left over at the end, which usually isn't as much as they'd hoped. The business is outwardly successful, but the owner isn't thriving. Instead of putting extra money in their personal bank account, they're making about the same—or less—than they did before they started the business. Combine this with working harder than ever before, and owners are in a tough spot.

This chapter is all about getting a good handle on the numbers so that you keep more of the money you work so hard to get. We'll dive into greater detail on finances in a later chapter, but before we go any further, it's important to talk about the basics.

## HOW TO SHIFT YOUR PRICING MINDSET

One of the fastest ways to increase your profits is to shift your mindset around pricing. Many owners have it in their heads that competing on price is how you win more customers. In our experience, the opposite is actually true. You want to sell based on value, not on price. Competing on price is a losing game because there will always be someone willing do the work cheaper.

What's more important, saving $10,000 on the sticker price of a new home while compromising on quality materials and skilled laborers, or having a well-built home that will withstand the test of time? The clients you really want will always choose higher quality and peace of mind over saving a small percentage on the price. When it comes to buying new construction, the amount saved ends up being negligible each month anyway when it is amortized over a 20- or 30-year mortgage. The sooner you get in the mindset of knowing that you don't want to be the cheapest, the sooner you'll start feeling more confident in pricing based on the excellent value you provide your customers.

Most potential customers aren't overly proactive about shopping around for the best price. We've sat with frightened custom home builders who were afraid that marking up their services by even a few thousand dollars would scare away prospects, when the reality was that most people wouldn't even notice the increase. In this industry, hardly any prospects walk away over a small percentage increase in price. If they are willing to do that, they are also probably willing to question every executive decision you make during the building process. In other words, they aren't the type of client you want anyway.

It's OK to charge more than what everyone wants to pay. Charging more to fewer paying customers is one of the easiest ways to improve your profitability. The secret to pulling this off is to identify the key prospects who can afford your prices and eliminate the ones who can't. When we tell coaching clients this, they often initially doubt that this strategy could work for them because they question whether they are worth the price increase.

Worthiness, as a builder or trade company owner, is a mindset. When you believe in the services your team provides, and you can confidently and honestly acknowledge that you are performing a high-caliber service, it makes pricing conversations much easier. Most of the time, when we ask business owners how their past work has been received, they respond that their clients were thrilled with the excellent results. But business owners may still get nervous when it comes time to talk about money. Just remember that charging what you are worth (even if it is higher than your local competitors) isn't the same as gouging. You have to believe in the quality of your work first before you can ever convince someone else to believe in it.

## HOW TO CREATE A SUSTAINABLE BUSINESS—THE 30,000-FOOT VIEW

Knowing that you don't want to compete on price is important because there is a good chance you'll need to raise your prices to become more profitable. For the vast majority of business owners we coach, expenses are higher than they realize, and they don't have an overview of how their numbers affect their profitability. You may feel that creating a sustainable business is about cutting costs, when in fact, the secret to profitability is raising prices. Examining your overhead is a great first step toward taking inventory of your business financials.

In this chapter, we will give you the 30,000-foot view of what needs to be considered in your profitability formula. It's important to get familiar with the key financial terms and metrics first, so you can understand why various sets of data are so important for your business. Ultimately, you will learn how to calculate certain formulas for yourself, including adjusting the numbers and knowing how various choices will affect your bottom line. But before you panic, know that you can do this. We work with business owners who aren't "math people" all the time, so if numbers are not your passion, don't worry. We have you covered.

## THE IMPORTANCE OF YOUR PROFIT AND LOSS (P&L) STATEMENT

Most business owners that we work with already have a P&L statement. Sometimes it's prepared by a bookkeeper or CPA, and other times it's automatically generated from accounting software, such as QuickBooks. Having this document is half the battle, and the other half is knowing what to do with it.

If you don't have a P&L, your priority lies in creating one— ASAP. It's critical to track your income and expenses so that you're able to understand how key numbers are related.

If you already have a P&L, that's great. This is the perfect time to get it out so you can reference it as you continue reading.

One of the first things that need to be identified on your P&L is the income and cost categories. It's important that you understand what these categories mean so that you can assess whether your expenses are being placed in the proper channels correctly. You would be amazed at how often we work with clients who misclassify their expenses. This can throw off all of the calculations of your P&L statement and create confusion as to what's really going on under the hood of your business. We will go into financial planning in more detail in chapter 11, but we want to cover the basics before we go any further.

Below are the categories in most P&L reports, along with their definitions.

- ❖ **cost of goods**: the amount paid for materials and labor used to build or remodel a home
- ❖ **expenses (also known as overhead)**: the costs of running a business, including rent, utilities, taxes, association fees, membership dues, office supplies, fuel, office staff, insurance, and marketing costs; are unrelated to project costs
- ❖ **gross profit**: the difference between income and cost of goods
- ❖ **gross profit margin (also known as gross profit percentage)**: financial gain expressed as a percentage of income (gross profit/income); not always shown in Quickbooks, but can be easily calculated
- ❖ **income**: money or revenue coming into a business.
- ❖ **net ordinary income**: the amount of money left over after cost of goods and expenses have been paid (income minus cost of goods minus expenses)
- ❖ **net profit margin (also known as net profit percentage)**: net ordinary income expressed as a percentage of income (net ordinary income/income); not always shown in Quickbooks, but can be easily calculated

## Sample P&L Statement

Here's an example of what a P&L statement in this industry might look like.

**ABC Builder, Inc.**
Profit & Loss
January 1 through December 31, 2020

| | Total Jan – Dec 2020 | Percentage of Income |
|---|---|---|
| **Income** | | |
| Smith Project | 467,000 | |
| Jones Project | 512,000 | |
| Andrews Project | 627,000 | |
| Collins Project | 558,000 | |
| **Total Income** | **2,164,000** | **100.00%** |
| Cost of Goods | | |
| Materials | 865,600 | |
| Labor | 129,840 | |
| Subcontractors | 735,760 | |
| Total Cost of Goods | 1,731,200 | 80.00% |
| **Gross Profit** | **432,800** | **20.00%** |
| **Expenses** | | |
| Lease | 36,000 | |
| Labor | 65,000 | |
| Officer Wages | 95,000 | |
| Utilities | 14,400 | |
| Travel | 5,500 | |
| Insurance | 6,000 | |
| Marketing | 24,000 | |
| Office supplies | 4,800 | |
| Accounting | 3,600 | |
| Total Expenses | 254,300 | 11.75% |
| **Net Ordinary Income** | **178,500** | **8.25%** |

## Quiz

Test your knowledge. How should the following costs be categorized? Refer to the key terms and definitions on p. 13–14, if needed.

1. 1,000 board feet of lumber
2. Two carpenters doing framing
3. Office rent
4. Mary's wages (whom you're paying to answer the phone and talk with clients)
5. Lease payments and fuel bills for project manager's company truck

Now that these definitions are fresh in your mind, go through your P&L report and check to see whether you have line-item expenses in the right spot. The main category to watch for is overhead. People often have things listed under overhead when they should really be categorized as cost of goods. It's common for this to happen if you pay people out of a payroll system.

Another common error we see in P&Ls is owners not including their own compensation as an overhead expense. You absolutely must prioritize your own salary. The number-one universally accepted reason for undertaking the challenge of starting your own business is to earn more income. Yet, many business owners become modest to a fault and pay everyone else instead of themselves. While this may seem altruistic, it is actually a very selfish business mistake.

If you can't afford to run the business and make it worth your while as the owner, eventually you will not be able to pay the people who depend on you for their livelihood. This is why you must build the business to be profitable for you first by factoring your salary into your overhead. This ensures that your business will support you financially, even in leaner times. Once you add in the salary you want to make, you can build a plan to achieve it.

**ANSWER KEY**
1. cost of goods
2. cost of goods
3. overhead
4. overhead
5. cost of goods

Go back through your P&L and see if any of these expenses need to be added or recategorized. If so, make the change in your accounting software and run the P&L report again.

## GROSS PROFIT MARGIN AND NET PROFIT MARGIN

It's important to minimize your overhead expenses and categorize as much as possible as cost of goods. This will give you the true gross profit for each job, since you will know what it *really* cost you to do each project.

Everything in cost of goods (lumber, supplies, labor, etc.) should be paid for by the customer on a project-by-project basis. Once you have all of those costs covered, you can accurately assess your overhead to determine how to calculate your margin. In other words, your overhead lets you know how much you need to "tax" on every revenue dollar coming in.

QuickBooks gives you the gross profit number but not the percentage, which is the gross margin. The gross margin is calculated by dividing the gross profit by the income.

A healthy gross profit margin is:

❖ 12 to 15 percent for spec home builds
❖ 15 to 22 percent for custom home construction
❖ 18 to 35 percent for remodeling

Net profit margin is calculated by dividing the net ordinary income by the total income. QuickBooks doesn't do this automatically, but it is easy to do it on a calculator.

Healthy net profit margins for any construction business should be 8 to 12 percent.

Take time to do this calculation now.

# REVENUE VERSUS PROFITS

There's one final point I want to address in this chapter, and it's an important one. When my team and I advise our clients that they should start raising their prices, you'd expect them to be ecstatic. Raising prices usually means that a business will earn more money. However, most of the time, our clients are very cautious about pricing themselves out of the market. Most are comfortable with a modest 10 percent gross margin. But this is too meager to get to the level of profitability that most businesses need in order to survive. Despite our field-tested "tried-and-true" approach, clients balk at our suggested 20 percent gross margin, which is a solid target for sustainable growth. We are used to hearing clients counter our figure with the *margin myth* that 10 percent is all the market will bear. But there simply isn't any truth to this scarcity mindset. In fact, it's actually possible to *earn less revenue* and *be more profitable.*

I once worked with a home building team that had this exact scenario play out for their company. The client was doing a high volume of about $8 million per year. Seeing that figure makes it seem like the business was successful, but behind the scenes, they were actually losing $200,000 per year. In other words, they were not making enough to cover their overhead expenses. This caused major conflict with the owners and team members because everyone was working harder but had nothing to show for it. One partner actually quit out of the blue right before we started coaching them.

When we looked into their financials, we found that they had four options for sustained long-term growth:

1. Reduce overhead expenses by at least $200,000
2. Raise prices to increase the gross profit by at least $200,000
3. Do a greater volume of work to increase profits at the current gross profit margin
4. A combination of all of the above

We decided that it made the most sense to hone in on increasing their profit margin. They were selling their services for only 12 percent gross margin. Using these numbers, we knew that they would need to earn an additional $1.67 million in revenue to cover the $200,000 loss ($200,000 / 12 percent).

The average price of one of their homes was $900,000, and

they told me that there was absolutely no way anyone would pay more. The fear of rejection scared them to death, yet paradoxically, this fear around charging their worth was the very thing that was crippling their business.

To begin turning things around, I asked them to raise their average home cost by $30,000, to $930,000 (14 percent margin instead of 12 percent). This number isn't that much higher in the grand scheme of things, but the client was still very reluctant. Finally, they agreed. Lo and behold, they sold just as many homes at 14 percent as they had been selling at 12 percent. When they saw that the small price increase didn't turn off their prospects, they felt the confidence to raise the margin to 16 percent.

The next year, they only earned $6 million in total revenue instead of $8 million, but, remarkably, *they made more money.* Increasing their margin caused their bottom line to go up dramatically. In fact, instead of *losing* $200,000 (like they had the previous year) they ended up *earning* a surplus of $200,000, even though their revenue was millions less.

This is the power of margin. It isn't greedy on behalf of a business or unfair to customers. Margin is a mandatory part of running a healthy company.

Many owners think that they should take on any job just to push their top-line revenue. Doing a certain amount of revenue can be a point of pride for business owners. It feels good to say your revenue is growing year after year. But focusing on your top-line growth is a good way to grow yourself out of owning a business. Your top-line revenue doesn't matter because you don't keep revenue, you only keep what is left over. To have more money in the bank, you need to focus on profitability instead of revenue. Knowing your numbers and how to maximize profit by charging what you're worth has the ability to radically transform your business. It is a simple shift that, once implemented, not only can help you survive as an entrepreneur, but empowers you to consistently thrive.

We'll dig a little deeper into finances in chapter 11, but this covers the basics. If you now understand how to categorize different types of expenses, you've achieved a major accomplishment in learning about profitability. If you learned the key numbers to look at on your P&L, and you know the relationship between those numbers, you've reached another huge milestone. As you get more comfortable and familiar with tracking the numbers in your business, you'll see that every number tells a story. When you get to know your numbers, you'll develop a greater understanding of how to make changes that will take you exactly where you want to go.

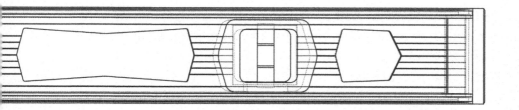

# CHAPTER 4

## LEADERSHIP AND CULTURE

All of our clients are leaders, but most don't think of themselves in that way. Instead, they see themselves as masters in their trade. When asked what they do, most reply something like this: *"I'm a builder."*

"I build custom homes."

"I'm in the home remodeling business."

Although many of these people have a team of employees and contractors who report to them, leadership isn't usually at the top of their list when they think about their job function. Instead, being a leader feels like more of a byproduct of owning the company. In fact, many owners feel like being in charge of a team is something that has almost been thrust upon them; they started their business because they were good at a trade, but as their business grew, they found themselves dealing with people much more than working with their hands.

It can be a tough reality that when you own a business, you become a leader, whether that was your intention or not. It's a totally different experience than wielding a hammer or laying drywall—and it requires a separate set of skills. Unless you came into the business and were given a full instruction manual on how to lead the people-side of things, or you went to school specifically for leadership and management, there's a good chance you've experienced a learning curve with that aspect of your role.

As the owner of your company, your job isn't just to oversee people and projects to make sure everything is running smoothly. You also need to create a vision, get people to believe in that vision, and gain their support in working toward shared goals. Your ability to do that has a huge impact on your success.

Owners in the construction and trade industries often think of company culture as a warm and fuzzy topic; it's something human resources people get excited about but everyone else can do without. If that resonates with you, know that you're not alone. A lot of our new clients have spent little to no time thinking about shaping their company culture. But when we begin coaching, we almost always uncover that culture is a major opportunity for meaningful improvement.

That's because every company—including yours—has a culture. Whether you were intentional in building a certain type of culture or not, your company has a unique feel that's unlike other businesses. It's baked into how things are run, the way in which people communicate with one another, the standards that team members hold themselves to in various aspects of their jobs, and more. If you haven't thought through your culture and set the rules of the game for your team, the team will play by its own rules. That's when businesses run into trouble.

As human beings, we're all different. The way I approach something might be different from how you'd approach it. Sometimes there is a clear right or wrong way to do something, but you'd be surprised how much of the world falls into a gray area. In many of those situations, people don't always know what they should do. We've worked with plenty of clients who were frustrated about how an employee handled something, and they couldn't understand why the employee would think that kind of behavior was OK. Oftentimes, this comes back to leadership and culture; employees aren't clear on what is expected of them. In those situations, who is really to blame, the confused employee or the owner who failed to provide guidance?

A lot of people like to take a hands-off approach to leadership and culture. They don't want to hover over their reports and tell them how to behave and why it's important. Although this kind of approach might come from a good place, it can have a negative effect because most employees look for someone to lead them. They want to do a good job, and to do that, they need guidance. This is true for both small tasks and big-picture direction. Employees want to know where the company is headed and how they fit into that vision. They want to know that there is a solid plan for the future, and that their boss isn't winging it.

When we work with clients and talk through this in our coaching sessions, we sometimes feel like we can almost see a lightbulb turn on over their heads. So many owners think their teams will be annoyed by receiving more direction on how to do things at the company. But the opposite is almost always true. Getting more-specific instruction can make your employees' jobs easier and more enjoyable.

## CORE VALUES

Core values are your company's North Star when it comes to setting the rules of the game and being intentional about shaping your culture. But when you're first starting out, and you have a small team, creating core values is an easy step to miss. (You're involved with virtually every aspect of the business, so why do you need to explain values that seem obvious, such as having integrity and doing your best work?) It might be smooth sailing at first, but when your company grows, you'll head into rough waters.

Every business owner wants certain things done in a specific way. Some of your preferences might seem intuitive (e.g., everyone should know that they need to speak to customers with respect), but employees don't always know how to navigate complex issues and competing needs. But if you have core values laid out, situations can be viewed through that lens as a litmus test for how to move forward; certain actions align with the core values, and others don't.

Core values are essential for guiding your team, and they can also help you stay on track aligning your actions with your vision for the company. Whenever you encounter difficult choices, you can refer to your core values to figure out your best path forward.

Our client, Musser Home Builders, is a great example of this. They have a fixed-price model for their contracts, where they run the risk of a decreased margin if projects come in over budget. Generally, this model works well for them, but when COVID-19 hit in the spring of 2020, the price of lumber and labor went sky high.

When we discussed this challenge with them, we asked if they were planning on making any adjustments to their existing contracts to address their increase in costs. The owner told us absolutely not. Since integrity is one of their core values, he said it would go against everything they believed in to go back and try to get more money out of their clients. Musser Home Builders is one of the most successful builders in its area, and the owner wanted to keep it that way. He said he would rather lose some money on a few builds that got caught in the price increase than lose his reputation.

We admired this commitment to the company's core values and saw how well they guided the decision-making process during a tough time that no one saw coming. That's exactly what core values are supposed to do. Although Musser was already in the red on a few homes, they nevertheless adjusted their pricing on all subsequent contracts to cover their increase in expenses, and were back on track in no time. It sent a strong message to both clients and employees that the company could be trusted to follow through on its word.

## CREATE OR UPDATE YOUR VALUES

If you don't have core values for your company, now is the time to create them. On the flip side, if you already have core values, now is the time to evaluate them and see if they still fit your business, and whether anything else should be added. Sometimes owners think values are set in stone, but in reality, they can—and should—be updated over time as the business grows. Here are a few tips:

**Research other companies' core values to help come up with ideas.** There are plenty of lists that will help your brainstorming sessions go much faster. Here are some examples to get you started:

Musser Homes

- ❖ **Relationship first:** Hands build homes, but hearts change lives.
- ❖ **Integrity always:** Innovative building with uncompromising commitment to traditional values.
- ❖ **Continually learning:** Expanding our experience by incorporating progressive technology and creative solutions as we mentor others.
- ❖ **Collaborative approach:** Establishing a culture of teamwork and collaboration within our company and with our trade specialists, our venders, and our clients.
- ❖ **Pursuit of excellence:** Passionate, forward-thinking, and detail-oriented, with an uncompromising approach to achieving outstanding results that last for a lifetime.

Small Business Growth Partners

- ❖ **Teamwork:** We are family 100 percent of the time.
- ❖ **Open and honest communication:** We can only address what is expressed.
- ❖ **Customer-centric focus:** We are the industry's best, and we show it.
- ❖ **Gratitude:** We are grateful for and appreciate one another all of the time.
- ❖ **Integrity:** We always do the right thing.

**Use your clients as inspiration.** Think about your top three to five clients—the ones you would want to work with every single day. What are their characteristics? What are they great at? These qualities might be a good fit for your own team's values. (What we admire in other people is what we value in ourselves.)

**Use your company's voice.** It's essential to word your values in a way that will resonate with your team. For example, "foster a spirit of unity" might not sound like something you or your colleagues would actually say, but "we're in this together" might sound more natural and capture the same sentiment.

**Be unique.** Your core values shouldn't be the same as everyone else's. If they sound generic and seem like what you might find on a stock image, you haven't dug deep enough. Your goal is to truly capture what's at the heart of your organization.

**Be honest.** Come up with values that fit your culture and goals, rather than values that just seem like something you should include. As an example, the retail giant Nordstrom does not have teamwork as a core value. Instead, they prioritize each employee's ability to help customers on an individual level. If you ever shop there, you'll probably notice that their culture aligns well with this value. This doesn't mean that Nordstrom is opposed to having their employees collaborate; it's just that other priorities trump teamwork, and that's totally fine.

**Ask your team for their input and feedback.** This is a great way to get your team involved in the process and gain their buy-in. If you already have core values, ask your team if your current values feel authentic to the business. If not, it could be that your values need to shift to match your culture, or that your culture has stopped following the North Star and you need to get back on track.

## HOW TO USE YOUR CORE VALUES

Coming up with your core values is the easy part. The hard part is integrating them into your company such that they align with your culture. Luckily, there are many ways to do this, but the key point is that your values should be used often enough that your whole staff knows what they are without having to look them up. When people are that familiar with what's most important at an organization, they can truly begin looking at their work through the lens of the values. That's where the magic happens. Here are a variety of ways to keep your values front and center:

**Rewards and recognition**: This is a best practice for engaging and motivating employees, but a lot of companies don't have their programs tied to their values as much as they should. When you incentivize people to take actions that align with the values, it's easier to get everyone rowing in the same direction. For example, you can ask employees to nominate their coworkers and share stories of how their coworkers are living the values. Each month, do a drawing of the people who were nominated and raffle off a prize. On top of that, set a goal for the number of nominations your whole team will get in a year and throw a celebration when the team meets it. These kinds of initiatives are not only positive reinforcement for a job well done, but they also add a bit of fun and excitement to the workplace.

**Meetings**: A great way to keep the values front and center is to make them a part of your regular team meetings. Hedlund Plumbing, a business that thrives on getting calls out of the blue to fix urgent problems, has had a lot of success with this by having an employee stand up at every meeting and talk about a core value and how it was reinforced with a client. Since implementing this best practice, they have seen a noticeable difference in having their staff unite toward common goals.

**Signage**: Having a visual reference of the core values is helpful, especially when people are first learning them. You can get them printed on just about anything, such as posters, virtual desktop backgrounds, coffee mugs, and more.

**Hiring**: Ask interview questions that get people to tell stories about how they have demonstrated some of your core values at their previous jobs (e.g., "Can you tell me about a time you acted with integrity, even though making the right decision was hard?"). Candidates' answers can give you a window into how well they would live these values at your company.

**Performance reviews**: An effective method for getting your team to take your values seriously is to tie their performance reviews to them. Employees should keep track of how their efforts have supported the company's values and share examples in their reviews. When you first start implementing this, it will become clearer who is a good cultural fit with the organization—and who's not.

**Firing**: Performance issues can be difficult to deal with, but core values make it easier to assess when someone has knowingly crossed the line. If people take actions that go against what you stand for as a company, don't feel bad about doing what needs to be done. Failing to act quickly can be damaging to your culture and demoralizing for your engaged employees.

**Marketing**: Share your values with clients and prospects so they know what you're all about. This can be done on social media and via general advertising, your website, and more. Talk about why your values are so important, and what that means for customers. (This will also help you attract job candidates that are a great cultural fit for your organization.)

# LEADERSHIP MINDSET

The main difference between leaders and managers is that leaders have people who follow them, and managers have people who work for them.[1] You want to be a leader, not a just manager. Although it's essential to manage the day-to-day aspects of the business, you can hire people to help with that. You can't outsource leadership. You have to step up and do it yourself, or you'll be sailing a ship with no one at the helm.

The thing that's tricky about leadership is that oftentimes it's not black and white. Unlike installing a faucet, there isn't one right way to do it. That makes it a lot harder to tell how

1. "Understanding the Differences: Leadership vs. Management," go2HR, October 4, 2021, https://www.go2hr.ca/retention-engagement/understanding-the-differences-leadership-vs-management

you're doing. And since you're the boss, your team might not feel comfortable enough to proactively give you feedback on how you're doing. That's why it's so important to show humility and make it clear to your team that you don't have the perfect answer for everything. Just like them, you are learning to be better at your job. You are trying your hardest, and you value their input so that you can continue to improve.

This attitude sounds simple, but so many people struggle to embody it. It takes vulnerability to be a good leader. You won't achieve it overnight. But if you work hard to have a leadership mindset when you're working in and on the business, you'll get things moving in a better direction and set yourself up for success when you scale.

One of the most important things you can do is gradually step out of day-to-day operations so that you clear time and mental space for your leadership work. It takes time and effort to make improvements, and you don't want to push those efforts to the back burner because you don't have the bandwidth to handle them. Most business owners are doing a lot of work that they could pay someone else to do, when, instead, they should be building a team that can operate without them. We always advise our clients to delegate and elevate. When you empower others to step up and manage various aspects of the business, it's a win-win for everyone.

If you think you could benefit from extra support to level-up your leadership skills, let your Small Business Growth Partners coach know. There are plenty of resources our team can share with you to help you succeed. That said, our best advice can be boiled down to something simple: The best leaders know they don't know everything, so they work hard every day to learn more. That's what it means to have a leadership mindset.

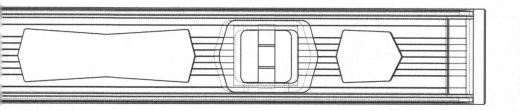

# CHAPTER 5

## SYSTEMIZING YOUR BUSINESS

When you first start your business, you do whatever it takes to grow it from the ground up. In the early stages, you wear multiple hats. You're responsible for juggling whatever tasks come your way and you're grateful to be able to work for yourself.

As you learn the ropes of your business, it's easy to find yourself focusing on the tasks right in front of you instead of thinking about how you can make your processes faster and scale your business in the future. In the early stages when your volume is low, if your operations are inefficient, it probably won't immediately impact your bottom line. In fact, chances are that you probably don't even realize how you could do certain things differently. At first, it's easy to meet all of your obligations, but as you grow, it becomes much more difficult to prioritize everything. As you expand and take on more employees and more complex projects, the consequences of not using smart, well-thought-out systems will start to catch up with you.

As an owner, you can't let your business just live in your head. You have to record how to do things so that you develop consistency in your operations and tasks can ultimately be done by other people. Without this kind of planning and forethought, you will always be chained to managing your company's operations instead of focusing on actually building your business. If your business depends 100 percent on you, and everything is in your head, what happens if you go down? Or want to take a vacation? Or even take a day off for your daughter's high school graduation?

Some people naturally think in systems, and some don't. The vast majority of business owners we know don't get out of bed in the morning thinking about their life and business as a collection of systems. So if you aren't a highly methodical person, don't beat yourself up. Most business owners have had to *learn* how to get good at systemizing their companies. It won't happen overnight, but if you are willing to do the work, it will make a huge impact in your business.

We won't lie to you. It takes extra time and effort to learn how to create systems and develop them. That's why a lot of business owners resist this process; it seems intimidating— and maybe even a little painful. But you know what? Systemizing your business is actually *liberating.*

## HOW TO CREATE GREAT SYSTEMS

Creating systems doesn't need to be difficult. In the beginning, this process can be as simple as sitting down and taking notes on how to complete the projects you do on a regular basis, whether it's daily, monthly, or even yearly. This serves two purposes. First, your notes become instructions that jog your memory later, which can be very helpful down the line after enough time passes and you're a little foggy on the details of specific projects. Being able to easily reference a go-to protocol for how to perform tasks can save you a lot of time and energy. Second, as your business grows and you delegate more of your tasks to others, your notes turn into a system anyone can follow. Since processes make it easy to get repeatable results, they allow your employees to duplicate your results and stellar performance.

To level-up your systems and make your operations even better, you should think about what you could you do differently to make your work faster and easier to do. Anything that gets completed more than once should be done as efficiently as possible. It might not seem like a big improvement to shave 5 or 10 minutes off a project by systemizing it, but when you implement that system every week for years, small improvements really add up.

Leveraging technology is another important part of creating efficient systems. A lot of builders and owners in the trade industries tend to do things the old-fashioned way rather than electronically (e.g., handwriting notes in a notebook or using a wall calendar). When it comes to systemizing, this is a recipe for failure. Electronic systems are almost always better than analog, even when they are extremely basic. To start, try creating templates for anything that can be copied and pasted in order to save your team time. You don't need to reinvent the wheel for things such as emails, proposals, change orders, schedules, scorecards, roles and responsibilities, selections, or FAQs. Next, let technology such as calendar alerts and CRM or project management software keep track of all the deadlines and daily operations and make it easier for you to communicate and collaborate with others. Inside these online tools, you (or your project manager) can create helpful calendars and reminder alerts, and even schedule follow-ups for clients and projects automatically.

## 13 SYSTEMS YOU NEED IN YOUR BUSINESS

Most builders only need to systemize about a dozen key processes to make a radical transformation in their operations. If you focus on getting these 13 systems in place first, it will make a world of difference to your entire business. Get out a pencil and record how well your company has implemented each of the following key systems by circling either "got it," "need it," or "needs more work" under each system below.

1. **Sales Process:** This includes the way you speak with prospects, explain your process, track follow-ups, and more. Developing a solid sales process is so important that we have a full chapter devoted to it (see chapter 9).

   ○ Got it    ○ Need it    ○ Needs more work

2. **Change Order Process:** This is the number-one margin killer in the home building industry. Oftentimes, customers will tell subcontractors or one of your team members that they want a different option or something moved from here to there. The trade partner or team member says "sure," but they don't tell the customer there will be a charge, and/or they fail to submit a timely invoice. There must be a process to prevent this miscommunication from happening and to make sure clients agree to changes in writing and are invoiced accordingly.

   ○ Got it    ○ Need it    ○ Needs more work

3. **Selections Process:** When customers choose their tile, carpet, and other details for a new custom home, it can be a tremendous amount of work to coordinate. If you don't have a solid system in place, this can easily waste a ton of time.

   ○ Got it    ○ Need it    ○ Needs more work

4. **Project Management Process:** In the beginning, a lot of companies wing the project management process and are then forced to get more organized later on when problems arise. If you can plan out a solid process ahead of time, it will save you countless headaches down the road.

   ○ Got it    ○ Need it    ○ Needs more work

5. **Punch List Process:** When customers have a laundry list of items that need to be handled at the end of a project, things can be easily missed if the process is unorga-

nized. You want to leave customers with an especially positive experience at this point in the relationship, so a solid process is key.

○ Got it    ○ Need it    ○ Needs more work

6. **Invoicing Process**: If invoices are not sent out the same way each time, it can be confusing for clients. This is something that can be easily outsourced via third-party software.

○ Got it    ○ Need it    ○ Needs more work

7. **Hiring Process**: When you hire employees or sub-contractors, you should go through the exact same onboarding steps every time. And if you have a solid process, chances are there are many steps. A system will ensure nothing gets missed, no matter how big or small the details, and no matter who helps onboard new team members.

○ Got it    ○ Need it    ○ Needs more work

8. **Scheduling Process**: This is another task that's likely done over and over in your business. It can become time consuming and cause issues on jobsites if it's not done well. Getting an organized process in place helps with everything from project management to employee satisfaction to customer service.

○ Got it    ○ Need it    ○ Needs more work

9. **Handoff Process**: When projects go from one stage to another—say, from sales to production and then from production to warranty—they get handed off to a different person or group of people who need to get up to speed on the details of the project. You want to make sure this is a smooth transition and that nothing gets missed.

○ Got it    ○ Need it    ○ Needs more work

10. **Post-project Reconciliation**: After a job is complete, it's essential to go back and determine how the actual project compares with the budget you initially set for it. Did it end up costing you more than expected, which made your margin lower than you intended? You should do this postmortem for every job.

    ◯  Got it      ◯  Need it      ◯  Needs more work

11. **Referrals/Testimonials Process**: This is the lifeblood for bringing in new business. You will have better results if you proactively ask for referrals and testimonials from your best clients. Make sure you aren't missing this important step in your business.

    ◯  Got it      ◯  Need it      ◯  Needs more work

12. **Strategic Alliance Process**: Partnering with other companies in your industry is a great way to get more high-quality jobs and work with people you like and trust. When you have a system in place for connecting with these kinds of firms—from architects to landscape design firms to real estate companies to relocation companies—it makes it much easier to keep this initiative going. These relationships will make a huge difference in not only your lead flow but also the quality of your prospects.

    ◯  Got it      ◯  Need it      ◯  Needs more work

13. **Staying In Touch Process**: Happy customers are a major asset for your business, whether they turn into repeat buyers or a source of referrals. But keeping in touch with people can be time consuming, and owners aren't often sure exactly what to say to past customers. A system for staying in touch—be it sending out regular mailings or a token gift, for example—can help you take the mystery out of the process and make it easy to execute over and over.

    ◯  Got it      ◯  Need it      ◯  Needs more work

14. Are there any other systems you realize you might need? Write them in the space below.

_____

_____

The nice thing about systems is that they can scale as your business grows. At first, they might be basic, but the beauty of having organized systems in place is that once you commit to writing them down, you can gradually add to them over time.

For instance, one of our clients, Jake Vierzen of R-Value Homes, mastered this concept of building out his processes gradually. R-Value Homes builds ICF (insulating concrete form) homes that are strong enough to withstand a hurricane. To provide this type of quality product and service to his customers, Jake has to be a high-energy guy. However, he is only one person, and as his business grew, he started to feel burned out. He knew he needed to become more organized and efficient about the processes in his business, so he hired a part-time office assistant and got to work focusing on systems.

Over the course of an entire year, Jake sat down every week and wrote down bullet points for how to complete certain processes in his business. Within one year, he had mapped out and documented the blueprint for how his entire business ran. He was able to hire people and easily train them, taking work off his plate and freeing up his time. Today, the business has grown and is more successful than ever.

## HOW TO DELEGATE, EMPOWER, AND OUTSOURCE

Every job that your company takes on means that you either have to do it or need to empower someone else to do it. As a business owner, you should always proactively think about how to delegate judiciously. One way to do this is to constantly ask yourself, "What can I pass along to other members of my team?" Owners should leverage their time to work *on* the business, instead of working *in* their business. Once you have systems in place, it makes it much easier for you to get the help you need.

To determine what types of tasks you should hand off, it's important to understand your strengths and what you enjoy doing. When you have something that falls outside those parameters into an area where you aren't as comfortable, you should delegate it to someone else. You also need to be able to recognize when certain tasks fall below your pay grade—even when they are quick and easy to do. Remember, your time is valuable, and paying someone else to do things will open the door to higher profitability because you are able to focus on the big-picture items that will ultimately make your company more profitable.

Once you start thinking this way, you will see how much better it feels to take items off your to-do list and put them on one of your employee's plates—and you go down this path, you will realize that about 80 percent of your business can be systemized. This will free you up to focus your energy where it counts: on growing your business, improving your company culture, and spending time with your family.

When you have clear and easy-to-explain processes, you can simply share the step-by-step breakdown with your employees so that they can do the work. This makes it easy to hold people accountable. Was the work done according to the documented procedure? This sets your employees up for success because they know what's expected. Remember, you're paying your team to follow instructions, not to read your mind. If your system lives only in your head, you are setting them up for failure, and setting yourself up for disappointment.

Don't forget to systemize new-hire training, too. A lot of owners forget that employees won't magically know how to do things right. You can quickly create useful training videos, folders with relevant documents, and links to helpful internal procedures that make it easy for your team members to get up to speed without you having to train them individually. Doing this will make it easy to share pertinent information with your team, and save precious time along the way.

Another important aspect of delegating effectively is knowing when it makes sense to outsource certain job tasks or functions to someone outside your company. Instead of getting too deep into things that are complicated, such as payroll, IT support, taxes, or HR processes, know that you can easily outsource them to a third party to save time. In the beginning, your system may be as simple as having a list of things to outsource and bullet points for how you want the work done. This can be all you need to start crossing tasks off your list.

## AIM FOR PROGRESS NOT PERFECTION

Systems are meant to evolve as you gain more experience and troubleshoot issues. One of our clients found this out recently with their scheduling process. Bob and Tom Hedlund own Hedlund Plumbing, a business that thrives on getting calls out of the blue to fix urgent problems. They were running into a major issue in their business because it was so hard to gauge how long it will take to fix customers' plumbing issues.

When Bob and Tom's plumbers would arrive on site, jobs were routinely much bigger than their customers realized. Since plumbing issues are often serious, the plumbers had to stay on the job until it was done, no matter how long and complicated it was. As a result, the plumbers were regularly late to the next-scheduled job, and those customers got upset. Bob and Tom found themselves constantly bogged down trying to meet their customers' needs while also managing their plumbers' unpredictable and fluctuating schedules. In other words, there was a serious flaw in the company's scheduling system.

After a while, the light bulb went off and the guys realized that they needed to do some troubleshooting. Even though their scheduling system worked when things went according to plan, they needed a fail-safe that allowed them some breathing room for when jobs took longer. Finally, they sat down and figured out how to make a minor tweak in their scheduling system, one that made a world of difference: They started scheduling their plumbers for only half a day instead of a full day. This way, if the plumbers showed up on the jobsite and the issue was time consuming to fix, they had time to do the work without throwing off the schedule later in the day. Best of all, plumbers were never overbooked.

Bob and Tom have used this system for years now, and it's genius. On some days, plumbers get to go home after a half day, but most days they end up working the full day. The most important thing is that customers are happy because their team shows up on time. It's also nice that the plumbers don't have to work overtime to complete jobs.

Bob and Tom's creative solution is a perfect example of building out processes and then improving them to deliver on what you promise. Every business will need a different solution, and most of the time, your systems will need some form of refinement to get it right.

Many entrepreneurs get stuck because they want to do things right the first time. But the reality is that no matter how simple your system is in the beginning, it's usually much better than nothing. Once you have a new process up and running, you can test, tweak, and refine it from there.

Improving your operations can take time, so get some help if you need it. In today's world, there is a goldmine of information available to you—just look for business solutions online. We also encourage you to set up a time to talk to your dedicated SBGP coach to get more help on how you can make specific improvements for your unique business. Your coach will be able to help you chart a game plan based on where you are right now. Keep in mind that things will evolve and get better over time.

Remember, your employees can actually be super helpful in assisting you with creating systems. In fact, when owners and colleagues come together to problem solve, it can help to smooth out tensions that arise between competing perspectives over the "right way" to do things; there is a preexisting accepted agreement already in place. The simple act of creating a process ensures that, as the owner, you don't get sucked into having to run all of the operations behind the scenes in your business.

## DON'T WAIT TO SYSTEMIZE YOUR BUSINESS

In Jim Rohn's *The Art of Exceptional Living,* he famously spoke about the paradox of gold miners who didn't want to "waste the time" to go buy a shovel. Instead, they tried to "maximize" their time by working nonstop. If you are so busy that you don't want to take time out of your schedule to create systems for your business, it's a lot like frantically digging for gold with your hands. A lot of gold slips right between your fingers.

While this example may seem silly, it is a reality for a lot of business owners. Sometimes, they have to get to the point where the frustration is unbearable before they are ready to create a better system. For many business owners, this frustration is never as acute as it is when they have to systemize their business in order to sell it or transition it to someone else. If they wait too long, it becomes nearly impossible to figure out. Not having clearly documented processes is the number-one killer of transitioning businesses. If everything lives in the owner's head, they won't be able to sell their business for a premium because someone else can't replicate their success.

When it comes to systemizing your business, the sooner you do it, the faster you will be on track to higher efficiency and enhanced profitability. If you wait until you get overwhelmed, you won't be in a good position to think strategically about the problems affecting your business; and being pressed for time will make things even harder. A best practice is to improve your business operations on an ongoing basis by carving out a little time each month to drill down on what works and what doesn't in your systems. The more you accomplish, the quicker you'll see results.

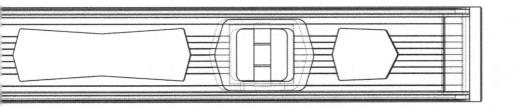

# CHAPTER 6

## HIRING AND ONBOARDING

Afew years ago, we worked with Mary, the owner of a remodeling company headquartered in Wisconsin. She prided herself on being highly self-sufficient and wearing multiple hats in her business. She was one of the most productive people we've ever met, but she was also stressed out all the time. Like many of the clients we coach, she was hesitant to hire somebody to do tasks that she could do herself. She had numerous internal processes that she felt she had perfected over the years, and she was fearful that someone else would not do as good a job as she did.

As we worked with her, she began to see that she had to make a change or she was going to burn out. She agreed to let go of some of her responsibilities and hire her first part-time employee. We all thought a bookkeeper would be an economical option to free up her time from doing work she wasn't overly passionate about anyway. So she went ahead and used our recommended hiring process to bring the bookkeeper on board.

What do you think happened?

After 15 years in business—15 years of Mary doing things

her way—the new bookkeeper was able to come in and make changes that actually *saved* the business money right off the bat. Yes, the bookkeeper covered his own salary *and then some*.

No matter how talented you are, there is always someone out there who can help you do the job better. Performing the nitty-gritty aspects of running a company actually keep you from growing the business, which ends up costing you money in the long run. We talked about this earlier in the book, but it bears repeating, especially since most of the clients we work with benefit from hiring at least one additional employee—right away. That said, a lot of owners don't know exactly what kind of role to hire for or how to properly go about the hiring process to get the best results. That's what this chapter is all about.

## GET CLEAR ON WHAT YOU NEED

How do you know when it is the right time for your company to expand? At SBGP, we use a term called *hiring triggers*. Hiring triggers are simple indicators that let you know when it is the right time to hire. The most common hiring trigger is when you want to start earning more but don't have enough employees to take on additional projects. Another trigger might be when you and your existing team feel overextended, and you worry about burnout or turnover. Yet another is when you have a lot of ideas to improve quality or service or convert more leads, but not enough time to implement them.

Recognizing that it's time to hire is the first step. From there, you need to get clear on what you need.

A lot of small businesses hire people they know, such as friends, family members, or local people in the community who are looking for work. This isn't necessarily a bad thing, but it narrows the talent pool considerably from the total population. And perhaps even more importantly, it can make them put the candidate's needs before the company's needs. For example, instead of figuring out what you need help with the most at your company, you try to find things Cousin Johnny could help with in the office. Maybe Johnny could someday evolve into your perfect office manager, but going about the hiring process that way isn't exactly going to fast-track your success. It would make a lot more sense to figure out which tasks you want to get help with, determine what skills and knowledge are needed to do those tasks, and then try to find someone who is well positioned to meet your needs. Maybe that's Cousin Johnny, or maybe it's not.

At smaller companies, defining new roles can be tricky, since employees wear a lot of different hats, and responsibilities can sometimes blend, depending on the needs at any given time. For instance, a single person might be in charge of overseeing certain sales opportunities, managing projects, and scheduling their own appointments. As the business grows, responsibilities should become more specialized so that people aren't doing such a wide range of tasks. The challenge is figuring out what this should look like in advance.

In construction companies, as well as in many trade businesses, the roles are pretty straightforward. The first person we almost always recommend hiring is a bookkeeper. Finding someone who can help you manage accounting by doing things such as invoicing, following up with clients, and basic bookkeeping will save you a tremendous amount of time. Additionally, it's usually easy to find someone for this role because it is an entry- to mid-level position that requires less skill and compensation than other roles within your company.

To help you navigate the chaos of managing projects, your company's second hire should mostly likely be a project manager. This person can help manage the day-to-day needs that so often become time consuming for you as an owner. One of the hardest aspects of hiring project managers is predicting how much capacity they will have, which can vary from person to person and from project to project. For construction businesses, project managers can typically handle anywhere from four to eight projects at once. If you are working on cookie-cutter production builds, that number may jump up to 20 or more. Again, this all depends on the complexity of the project.

Once you have these main roles covered, you may want to bring on additional people to fill other important positions: a selections coordinator (for construction businesses), an estimator, an administrative assistant or office manager, and a salesperson.

A great way to help decide whom to hire is by assessing your current workload and thinking about what you enjoy and what you're good at. Anything that doesn't fall into those two buckets is something that someone else should ultimately do.

# HOW TO CREATE JOB DESCRIPTIONS AND JOB ADS

Once you determine the roles you need to hire for, your job is to communicate those needs to others. Your inclination might be to go ahead and start writing a job ad you can post ASAP, but that would be jumping the gun. Before you can condense the opportunity into a few emotionally engaging paragraphs that make people want to drop everything and apply for that role, you need to have a better understanding of what the job actually entails.

This is where the job description comes in. It isn't as sexy as the job ad, but it's monumentally important for helping new hires get started and perform at a top level right away. When you flesh out all the details of a role (including key responsibilities and expectations) and clearly communicate them, you define what success looks like for that job—and people will be much less likely to disappoint you once they're hired because they'll already understand what they need to do.

After you've done the hard work of creating a solid job description, the job ad can be developed from there. The ad is more of a marketing piece that helps you sell the applicant on the company and the role. You need some details on what the job entails, but not as many as the job description. Instead, you should include a well-crafted description of the company, the benefits and perks that come with the job, and what type of employee would fit well within your company culture. This is where you really want to sell the company and make the role sound attractive to potential prospects. Most companies we work with have some room for improvement in this regard. Remember that marketing for new employees is no different from marketing to potential customers: It's 80 percent emotion and 20 percent logic. Make sure to spice up your ads so people know that your company is a fun and exciting place to work. The goal should be to make people want to pursue a career with your company, and not just go after another paycheck.

Once your job description and job ad are polished and proofread, you'll need to determine the best marketing strategy. Your own network is always the first place you should start because it is usually your best source. If you're looking for new team members, let your network know. Tell your current team, your friends, and people in your community. (This is where you can share the job ad with Cousin Johnny—and any number of other people in your network—to start the process of determining who is the best fit.)

Many business owners make the mistake of only looking for applicants who are currently unemployed. Sometimes, your best hire could be already employed. That's why you want to get the message out far and wide so that people who are already employed, along with those who are actively looking for work, know you are hiring and can then take the initiative to approach you.

Ideally, marketing for new people should be an ongoing process. Think about building your team just like fielding a professional sports team. General managers are always keeping an eye out for the best talent in the league. That way, when they're interested in adding to the team, they already have some idea of people who might be a good fit. Your company should approach hiring the exact same way.

Always keep your options open; you should have a standard hiring page on your website. Explain why your company is a great place to work and include video testimonials from current employees. It's simple to share this link on social media sites such as Facebook and LinkedIn when you are looking for new talent. By doing this, you will create an evergreen marketing strategy so that when you need to hire someone fast you have a pool of talented prospects already at your disposal.

# HOW TO SUCCESSFULLY CONDUCT AN INTERVIEW

Interviewing your job applicants well is crucial to making the best hires. The quality and thoroughness of your interview process is the difference between hiring the right person who stays with your company for decades and the *almost right hire* who stays on for only two weeks and frustrates your current team in the process.

Start by figuring out what you really need to know from your applicants. Use your past experience with employees and how they handled difficult situations as a starting point. The best strategy is to let your interviewee do most of the talking. Ask open-ended questions aimed at uncovering their experience and approach to the role.

Sometimes, interviewers feel like they need to talk people into taking the job. Don't be desperate. Waiting for the right person who is the best fit is always better than hiring a warm body off the street.

To ensure that we always have questions ready to go, we at SBGP ask questions based on 21 categories. Some of our categories include *decisiveness, safety awareness, motivational fit, ability to learn, work tempo, adaptability,* and *attention to detail.* Our interviewers never talk too much or go off-script because they have everything they need to get a complete picture of who the applicant is and what they are capable of. Why? Because we prioritize asking high-quality questions to receive high-quality responses during our interviews.

## DISC IMPLEMENTATION

The DISC assessment was created by Dr. William Moulton Marston, a lawyer and psychologist who shared the DISC model in his 1928 book *Emotions of Normal People*. Marston conducted research on human emotions, and based on those findings, postulated that people illustrate their emotions using the behavior types of Dominance (D), Inducement (I), Submission (S), and Compliance (C), or DISC for short.

By using these assessments in our hiring practice, we can identify the predictable aspects of behavior and communication and use that knowledge to help us select the best candidate to hire. The assessment results provide insight into behavioral tensions, causes of stress, problem-solving, and ways the candidate may respond to conflict and job situations.

The assessment industry is largely unregulated and DISC is what's termed "open-source research." This means anyone can produce an assessment and call it a DISC profile. As a result, the scientific accuracy of DISC profiles varies widely. We recommend considering only DISC profiles that have published validity and reliability studies. For this reason, SBGP acquires all their assessments from Assessments 24x7. To learn more about this great company, explore their website: assessments24x7.com.

The DISC model uses four behavioral reference points. A formal assessment goes much deeper, but here is an overview of the four styles:

| DISC Focus | Problems/ Tasks | People | PACE or Environment | Procedures |
|---|---|---|---|---|
| **Needs** | Challenges to solve, Authority | Social relationships, Friendly environment | Systems, Teams, Stable environment | Rules to follow, Data to analyze |
| **Fears** | Being taken advantage of/loss of control | Being left out, loss of social approval | Sudden change/loss of stability and security | Being criticized/loss of accuracy and quality |
| **Emotions** | Anger, Impatience | Optimism, Trust | Patience, Non-Expression | Fear, Concern |

Reviewing a job applicant's DISC results helps you learn how well they will mesh with your current team before they ever step foot in your office for an interview. It also empowers you to ask more-pointed questions that will get you better answers. Another benefit of asking people to complete an assessment *before* the in-person interview is that it shows you how bad an applicant wants the job. If they're willing to do this extra step, it's a good indication of their motivation.

Certain types of positions will skew toward a specific DISC profile. For example, most experts recommend that a salesperson be an I or a D profile. However, some of our clients have successful sales teams that have all C's if they are selling a technical product. Accountants and project management may also be a good fit if they have a C or S profile. Just be aware that you'll always find a unicorn who doesn't fit the mold. What really matters is how you want a job done and matching that to a DISC assessment.

One of our clients specifically used DISC to successfully fix their high turnover rate. The whole team at Waukesha Graphics would get fired up about a new hire, only to have them last just 90 days. It was demoralizing for their entire staff. We coached them through the process of working with their DISC assessment to help guide their hiring process. The next time they were ready to pull the trigger and hire someone, they had the potential candidate take the assessment beforehand. Based on the results of the assessment, we guided the client on which key questions to focus on in the interview. This helped them get specific with whom they went after so that they only hired the best candidate. After implementing this simple change, their attrition rate was cut in half. Today, Waukesha Graphics has 20-plus loyal employees, whom they've built their company's culture around, because they prioritized hiring people who were committed to growing with the company.

Based on our client data, the success of companies that use DISC in their hiring process, such as Waukesha Graphics, isn't unique. We've found that when employers implement DISC assessments prior to hiring, it doubles the odds of retaining their employees.

## DEFINE THE HIRING PROCESS

Often companies don't have a process in place for when a new employee joins the team. Being proactive and setting clear expectations up front is vital to employee success. Our method follows a simple eight-step approach. Once we have the job description and job ad completed, we post the job opening to various social media and job sites for wide exposure. Then, we start screening the applications that come in to select only the top candidates for a phone screen. Our phone screens are a relaxed, 30-minute conversation with questions that are fairly thorough. Once an applicant progresses past a phone screen, it's time to invite them into the office to meet the team and have an in-person interview. Once the in-person interview is confirmed as on the books, we ask them to complete a DISC assessment. As a team, we spend a lot of time prepping for the interview and creating specific questions tailored to their individual DISC profile. After their interview, we select our favorite candidate and present an offer. If their mandatory pre-employment checks look good, we coordinate a start date and welcome our new team member to their new work family.

It's that simple.

| STEP | STAGE | TASK | OWNER | STATUS |
|---|---|---|---|---|
| 1 | POST JOB OPENING | **Four Tasks** | | |
| | | Create/review/revise JOB DESCRIPTION. | | o |
| | | Use Job Description to create/review/revise JOB POSTING. | | o |
| | | Upload Job Posting to job board sites. | | o |
| | | Use other recruitment strategies as needed: social media posts, employee referral bonuses, etc. | | o |
| 2 | SCREEN RESUMES/APPLICATIONS | **Three Tasks** | | |
| | | Compare applications against Job Posting requirements. | | o |
| | | Select the top three to five candidates for PHONE SCREEN. | | o |
| | | Create/review/revise PHONE SCREEN FORM. | | o |
| 3 | PHONE SCREENS | **Three Tasks** | | |
| | | Conduct PHONE SCREEN using Phone Screen Form (30 minutes). | | o |
| | | Select top two to three candidates for IN-PERSON INTERVIEW. | | o |
| | | Schedule In-Person Interviews with each candidate. | | o |
| 4 | IN-PERSON INTERVIEWS | **Four Tasks** | | |
| | | Create/review/revise INTERVIEW GUIDE as needed for the position being filled. | | o |
| | | Determine format/logistics of interview (who, where, when, how, etc.)? | | o |
| | | Conduct IN-PERSON INTERVIEW using Interview Guide (45 to 90 minutes, depending on position). | | o |
| | | Select top candidate. | | o |
| 5 | DISC ASSESSMENT | **Two Tasks** | | |
| | | Send DISC ASSESSMENT to top candidate. | | o |
| | | Review DISC assessment report and make final decision. | | o |
| 6 | PRESENT OFFER | **Two Tasks** | | |
| | | Prepare CONTINGENT JOB OFFER. | | o |
| | | Notify candidate and collect contact info for REFERENCES. | | o |
| 7 | PRE-EMPLOYMENT CHECKS | **Four Tasks** | | |
| | | Schedule candidate's pre-employment drug screen. | | o |
| | | Conduct background check(s) as required. | | o |
| | | Conduct Employment Reference check(s). | | o |
| | | Determine final disposition of candidate based on pre-employment checks. | | o |
| 8 | START DATE | **One Task** | | |
| | | Notify candidate and determine start date. | | o |

# SET UP EXPECTATIONS FOR ONBOARDING

For a lot of companies, onboarding is just a term to describe the first couple of weeks a new person is on the job. Unfortunately, this perspective is exactly what sets companies up for new-hire failure. Rather than just a moment in time, onboarding should actually be an intentional practice where a company goes the extra mile to help new team members get acclimated and set them up for success. This includes teaching new hires how to perform their work tasks, introducing them to their colleagues, setting expectations for their performance, and more. If companies skip these steps and assume new hires are mind readers, things will not go well. The biggest mistake we see is when employers don't communicate what they want out of their new hires.

For example, we had a builder named Jeff who hired a general laborer named Charlie. Charlie's performance wasn't cutting it and Jeff was ready to place Charlie on a performance improvement plan (a specific plan that details what someone needs to do in what timeframe to meet the requirements of the position), or let him go if he didn't rise to the challenge. But when Jeff called Charlie into his office, Jeff realized that no one on his team had told Charlie what was expected of him. He had never received a job description, and he no idea he was expected to tidy up his work area or proactively look for things to help with during down time. He assumed that as long as the work got done he could relax in between tasks. He wasn't doing a good job because they never discussed what a good job looks like. After their discussion, Jeff knew that Charlie's performance was a direct result of poor onboarding, which was the company's fault. Charlie became a top producer (virtually overnight), and has done a stellar job ever since then.

To achieve effective onboarding at your company, all you need is a little intentionality, logic, and organization. Never forget that new hires *want* to know what's going on. They not only hope you will walk them through all the major processes and systems to do their job, they also want to know about the company overall. They are eager learners, so teach them how to uphold the integrity of the organization—and its culture. Show the warmth of the team by going the extra mile to make them feel at home. Supervisors should give new hires a hand-written welcome card. This goes a long way toward building rapport and showing new hires they are in good hands.

Lastly, build in opportunities to circle back and check in with new hires to see how they're doing. This gives them the opportunity to ask questions that they might have been too shy to bring up on their own.

Hiring can be one of the most challenging areas for any construction or trade business, but there are also plenty of opportunities to take this part of your business to the next level. As you think back on the tips in this chapter, reflect on what your company might be able to do to improve the hiring process. Whether it's getting clear on what your next open position will be, writing a job description, or familiarizing yourself with DISC, there are plenty of ways that small improvements can make a resounding impact. Over time, it will get easier to consistently achieve the goal all business owners share: keeping new hires around for many years to come.

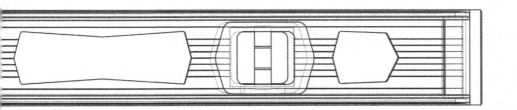

# CHAPTER 7

## MANAGING EMPLOYEES
## AND CONTRACTORS

When your business grows and you have more people on board to help get the work done, it seems like your job should get easier. In many ways, it does. But a lot of owners find themselves struggling with the additional work of managing a team while still being constantly sucked in to answering questions and evaluating details they hoped would be handled by someone else.

For many builders and trade business owners, this is a challenging spot. Most of our clients got into the industry because they were good at building houses, hardscaping, plumbing, or just about anything other than managing people. And yet, when they hone their craft and grow their business, more and more of their time is spent on management—something many don't necessarily enjoy or feel well prepared to do.

Luckily, there are a few best practices you can focus on to really boost your success in motivating, engaging, and retaining a strong team that will add value to your company and ultimately make your job easier.

# THE FOUR LEADERSHIP STYLES OF SITUATIONAL LEADERSHIP

It's difficult to strike the right balance of teaching and helping your team members get things done versus leaving them on their own. If you're too far on either end of the spectrum, it creates issues. That's why we're huge proponents of the Four Leadership Styles of Situational Leadership.[2] This model shows how your leadership style and habits should change over time depending on the situation.

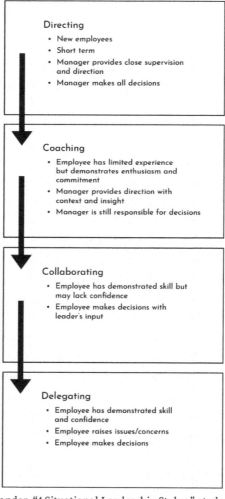

Directing
- New employees
- Short term
- Manager provides close supervision and direction
- Manager makes all decisions

Coaching
- Employee has limited experience but demonstrates enthusiasm and commitment
- Manager provides direction with context and insight
- Manager is still responsible for decisions

Collaborating
- Employee has demonstrated skill but may lack confidence
- Employee makes decisions with leader's input

Delegating
- Employee has demonstrated skill and confidence
- Employee raises issues/concerns
- Employee makes decisions

2.   Todorov, Alexander, "4 Situational Leadership Styles," atodorov.org, November 11, 2017. http://atodorov.org/blog/2017/11/11/4-situational-leadership-styles/

1. **Directing:** When you're working with new hires, you need to provide more directive support. In other words, you tell people exactly what they need to do, and check in on them and review their work. This helps people understand what's expected of them so they know whether they are delivering what's needed. It's a hands-on style of management that works well for getting people up to speed.

2. **Coaching:** As your team gains more experience, the way you manage them should change. You become better able to back off and let them do more on their own. Instead of telling people exactly what to do, you're coaching them through projects as they make more decisions independently. But before you loosen the reins too much, you need to explain more of the "why" behind things being done a certain way so that you can get employees' buy-in. This is the stepping stone to enabling them to think more critically and start making decisions using the methodology you've taught them.

3. **Collaborating:** This style is fundamentally different from styles 1 and 2 because it's driven by the follower instead of the leader. At this point, employees have most of the knowledge to complete their work, but they might not have the confidence or experience to do it totally on their own. As the leader, you listen to employees' recommendations for how to move forward with various challenges and weigh in or offer feedback as needed. You're a resource for your team as they lead projects.

4. **Delegating:** Here's the style that you're probably looking forward to the most. In this style, employees are fully competent and confident, and they excel at performing their job duties autonomously. As the leader, you aren't involved in the vast majority of work your employees perform because they can do it well on their own. You assign new projects and your team gets them done without much direction, coaching, or support. That said, it's

important to note that delegating is different from abdicating. Even when your team is high functioning and they do a great job of managing tasks without oversight, as the owner, you are still the primary person responsible for your team's output. That means you still need to monitor all work—to some degree.

These four styles work best when they are a part of a journey, where employees learn their job duties in a supportive environment and gain a solid understanding of what's expected. This process helps them feel empowered and enables them to keep learning and growing in their role. When they're ready to take on more, they'll have the autonomy to do so, and they won't be bottlenecked by a boss who wants to review and micromanage every little thing.

On the flip side, this model is also ideal for you, as the leader. When you invest your time up front in making sure people are well prepared to perform at their highest level, you reap the rewards for years to come. Your team can function effectively without over-relying on you, and you don't have to continuously be involved in the nitty-gritty details that are, quite frankly, below your pay grade.

Unfortunately, most leaders do not excel at implementing all four of these styles. The majority are only comfortable with one or two. With this in mind, it should come as no surprise that when we work to improve how builders and trade business owners manage their teams, we usually hone in on a point in one of these four styles where things break down.

Many clients' greatest problems happen right away with new employees. Instead of starting at style 1 (directing), they jump forward to style 3 (collaborating) or even style 4 (delegating). New hires are simply not ready to become self-sufficient so early in the process, so this is a recipe for disaster. As we discussed in the previous chapter, you need to properly onboard your team members so that they can get their bearings, learn what's expected, and ultimately be able to exceed your expectations in their role. All of this takes time.

Another common issue we see is when leaders don't progress through all four styles and instead get stuck somewhere in styles 1 to 3 with employees who are more than capable of working autonomously. The reality is that at some point you have to let go, coax your little fledglings from the nest, and let them figure things out on their own. Otherwise, it's easy to fall into the trap of *upward delegation*, where you help employees so much that they begin to rely on you instead of thinking through solutions on their own. As a leader, when you have numerous people doing this on a regular basis, it can make it nearly impossible for you to have time to do anything else.

I had this issue many years ago in another business, and I felt like I always had a line outside my office of people who wanted me to come up with answers to their problems. I decided to put a sign on my door that said, "One question: Two answers." I told my team that this sign meant they could only come to me with a question if they had already thought of two possible answers, or solutions, on their own. At that point, they were welcome to knock on my door and share their question and two potential answers so we could talk through the situation and I'd give them feedback. I wanted them to know that they

> **REFLECTION**
>
> *Think about your natural style of leadership. Where does it tend to fall within the four styles? Maybe you're strong in a couple of styles, but weak in others. Think about how your approach to leadership aligns with your employees and subcontractors. Should you be offering more support to certain individuals? What about backing off and letting some people make mistakes and learn on their own?*
>
> *Write down a couple of things you can start doing differently today to better meet people where they are. The more you can tailor your approach in unique situations, the more success you will find in becoming an effective leader.*

should consult with me on important issues but at the same time feel empowered to solve lower-level problems on their own. Soon after my sign went up, the line outside my office started to shrink. After a couple of months, the team had gotten into such a great habit of evaluating potential solutions that I was rarely asked to consult on their issues anymore. My team and I have shared this trick with numerous clients who have successfully instituted it at their own organization, whether for in-person questions or virtual.

# CONNECT WITH EMPLOYEES

A few years ago, one of our coaching clients was having a sudden problem with turnover. As a successful custom home builder with more than 15 years of experience, it seemed like he had cultivated a strong team of people who were committed to the company. But then one top performer quit, and then another, and another. The owner tried hard not to go into panic mode, but it was a major problem for a small team to lose so many people in close succession.

We told him about the leadership strategy called *managing by walking around*. It's incredibly effective in a variety of industries, including automotive, healthcare, manufacturing, and, of course, construction and the trades. The idea is to go on-site and talk to employees and subcontractors in their work environment. This gives leaders a chance to see what job conditions are really like in a variety of roles, and the kinds of challenges team members run into on a regular basis.

So our client followed our advice and visited his jobsites to get to know his team members better. He asked what the company could do to better support workers, how he could help them in their current roles, and what their long-term career aspirations looked like. He made an effort to get to know people on a personal level, rather than just understanding what they could produce for him in a professional capacity.

He was surprised to learn that job conditions were not as favorable as he had once believed. He had plenty of experience building homes, but at that point in his career he wasn't in the thick of it day after day. He didn't realize there were hiccups in the company's processes that slowed things down and caused frustration for his team. People weren't communicating as well as they should have, and certain policies were causing confusion. After speaking with employees and subcontractors, he could see why some of his team members had decided to leave the company.

Immediately, the owner went to work to fix the concerns he learned about on the jobsites. After the changes were made, he went back and visited employees again to tell them directly that he appreciated their feedback and had implemented changes because of what he'd learned. Workers seemed shocked, to put it lightly. Most of them hadn't seen the owner in ages, and all of a sudden, there he was showing up like a true leader.

That was a turning point for the organization. The owner realized that an open-door policy doesn't mean anything if people don't feel comfortable using it. To really get to know your team and understand their needs, you need to proactively ask them questions about their job, and not be afraid of their answers. Since instituting the *managing by walking around* philosophy, our client's turnover issues are behind him, and the company is doing better than ever.

We highly recommend that you try this type of management at your organization. To make sure that it gets done on a regular basis, you will need to schedule it in your calendar. You might also need to schedule time to follow up on any action items that result from talking with employees directly. This is a crucial aspect of making this effort actually work; you must take feedback to heart and drive real change. This doesn't mean you need to make adjustments you don't believe are truly needed, but you do need to follow through on what you say you're going to do and work to build trust and rapport with your team members.

# HOW TO MANAGE AND EVALUATE PERFORMANCE

A lot of the builders and trade companies we work with only have a few employees. This is one reason why so many of them have a casual—or nonexistent—performance evaluation process. There might be conversations about pay or performance from time to time, but it's sporadic and often undocumented.

Whether you've had the same team for decades (and they're your family members) or you just hired people you met recently, it's important to have a solid system and routine in place for managing and evaluating performance. The foundation of this is documenting what your expectations are. It doesn't work to simply verbalize it and expect people to remember. That's why the job description we covered in the last chapter is so important to have for every role. You need something to point to when it comes to performance so that everyone is on the same page.

A key element to making a performance evaluation system work is frequency. If you have yearly reviews, that leaves 364 days when no one talks about performance. But if you have weekly check-ins, you get into a rhythm where the whole team keeps it top of mind.

Everyone in the company should have KPIs they are responsible for and need to track on a regular basis. KPIs work best when they are tied to something measurable such as the number of meetings with prospective clients or the number of days a project is ahead or behind schedule. Each KPI should have a target that can be tracked weekly. These numbers get put into weekly reports called "scorecards," which are shared with managers. Scorecards are especially helpful for your numbers-driven sales team, which we will get into in greater detail in chapter 9. However, employees don't have to be responsible for sales in order to find metrics that make sense to tie to their performance. For example, maybe your project managers should aim to have 95 percent of their projects be on schedule. A bookkeeper's goal could be to have 100 percent of invoices sent on time, and 90 percent of payments received on time. A person's KPI might be to have a certain percentage of choices made before specific milestones during the project.

Sometimes it's tricky to come up with the KPIs that make the most sense for various roles, so put some thought into what matters most so you can track them and help your team stay accountable.

Make sure you're tying elements of your performance evaluations to your company's core values. (If one of your values is giving customers a great experience, determine which job duties relate to that in every role and track your team's success in delivering on those tasks.) Prioritizing your core values in every person's performance is a smart way to keep the whole team rowing the boat in the same direction. It also helps people feel like they are part of something bigger than themselves and connects them to the overall purpose of the business and how they fit into that picture.

Finally, if you don't already have an employee handbook, now is the time to create one. This document is the perfect place to house all of the information your team needs. From core values to rules, policies, and culture, a handbook goes a long way in making sure everyone understands expectations. Once you create your handbook, keep it updated on a regular basis.

## MANAGING SUBCONTRACTORS

Nearly all companies in the construction industry rely on subcontractors for certain aspects of their projects. It can be a unique situation, especially since clients are often unable to differentiate between your employees and those who are subcontracted through other companies. It's important that your subs are properly trained and showing up in the way you want. Make sure you educate them on your culture and rules, and on what's most important at your organization. Share sections of your handbook to save time and streamline this process.

You wouldn't have the same career advancement conversations with subcontractors as you would with employees, but you should still ask them for feedback on how projects are going and input on whether there is anything that could be changed to work better together. A best practice is to have standing meetings twice a year with your key subcontractors to talk through what's working and what isn't. Getting into a rhythm with this kind of conversation goes a long way in building high-functioning relationships where both parties feel valued. Don't ever forget that people do business with people they know, like, and trust. When the industry goes through challenging times and there are labor shortages, you want to have a leg up keeping your top subcontractors.

## MANAGING CONFLICTS

Performance isn't usually a pressing issue if your team is committed, talented, and living your core values. However, we all know that business isn't quite as rosy as this ideal. When a conflict arises or someone on your team isn't performing up to your standards, it's up to you to do something about it—quickly. The longer you let issues go on, the worse they will become.

Refer back to the DISC assessment your team members did when they were first hired and consider how their results play a role in their behavior. Are team members failing to see eye to eye because they come at issues from totally different perspectives? Maybe miscommunication could be easily resolved with a candid conversation. DISC provides a wealth of tools for managing interpersonal conflict, so make sure you utilize those resources, and encourage your team to proactively do the same.

When issues surpass simple conflicts and turn into real performance challenges, you need to deal with them as soon as possible. One key reason for this is other team members will see what's happening. We strongly believe in the saying, If you permit it, you promote it. If you allow one employee to get away with certain things or allow them to not pull their weight, other employees will also think it's OK. And those who don't lower their personal standards will become bitter that the employee in question is able to get away with poor performance. This brings down productivity and morale for everyone. So as uncomfortable as it can be to have direct conversations with employees about their performance, it's a non-negotiable part of being a business owner. When you have a job description, core values, and scorecards in place, it makes it much easier to have objective conversations and let people go when they are no longer a good fit.

## PROVIDING FINANCIAL INCENTIVES

Cultivating a positive environment that makes people want to come to work is a key part of becoming an employer of choice, but we can't ignore financial incentives. People want to be paid well for their work. There are a lot of variables at play here to determine what good compensation looks like, such as roles and responsibilities, experience, average wages in your local area, and fluctuations in the cost of living. The best practice we recommend is to be in the top 25 percent of companies in your industry and area. It's worth it to pay a premium for good employees. You don't ever want people to leave because of pay, and if rates are in the top 25 percent, it makes it much less likely you'll have turnover because of compensation.

You might also want to consider bonuses to attract and retain employees. One of our coaching clients was scared they would lose some of their team members because a competitor was offering a $2,000 signing bonus. For their landscaping businesses, which does a ton of work over the summer, it would have been terrible to lose key team members right when business was picking up. We advised them to offer a "stay" bonus. If employees stayed through the end of the season, they would get $1,000. This ended up being the perfect solution to retain their team from the previous summer.

For higher-level long-term employees, financial incentives might include a small percentage of ownership in the company. That might sound scary if you've never considered it, but hear us out. One of our coaching clients had two key employees they were worried about losing. They had worked at the company for more than a decade, but it seemed like their enthusiasm was starting to lose its luster. The owner gave them each a 2 percent ownership in the company and created a program through which they could earn more ownership based on key milestones. This really changed the dynamic for both employees. They felt valued and became more emotionally invested in the business. Their performance increased, and years later, they're still with the company.

Building a productive, effective team doesn't happen overnight, but it's well worth the hard work and effort. As you develop your people-management skill set, remember that no one starts off knowing exactly what to do. Growing a team can be a messy and imperfect process, and that's OK. The more intentionality you put into improving your capabilities, the better you will become.

The most important thing is to show your team that you're trying. Be humble, ask for feedback, and demonstrate that you are committed to them. When you do those simple things, you will earn your team's commitment and respect in return.

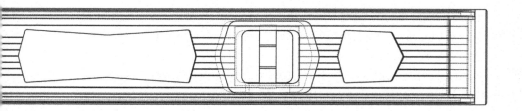

# CHAPTER 8

## MARKETING

A lot of our clients tend to think of sales and marketing as a single endeavor, but they are actually two very different business elements. The goal of marketing is to get people in your target market to raise their hand, want to learn more about you, and show interest in buying. Sometimes that happens immediately, and sometimes it takes years of exposure across a variety of mediums. Once people raise their hand, interactions with them are considered sales rather than marketing. This process is like an internal baton pass.

Every business owner's goal is to perfect marketing and get the right kind of leads coming in at the optimal volume and cadence. This sounds pretty straightforward on paper, but we all know it's easier said than done. Luckily, there are some simple ways to make your marketing efforts easier to manage—and more effective. In this chapter, we'll cover the most important things you need to know about improving your marketing so that you keep your sales flowing in the right direction.

### SCALABILITY

The great thing about marketing is that it's highly scalable if done properly. Some companies thrive with little to no marketing, while others invest heavily in a variety of mediums and get even more in return. When it comes to builders and trade companies, we tend to see a lot of confusion around choosing how much time and money to invest and deciding where to focus.

Most builders only need to spend 1 to 3 percent of their annual revenue on marketing. This is much less than companies in most other industries spend, for one simple reason: The average dollar sale per transaction is comparatively much higher. It isn't like running an ice cream shop where the owners need 200 people to buy scoops each day just to break even. Most of the builders we work with have a max capacity of around 10 to 20 homes per year. Trade businesses that have lower average dollar sales tend to spend a greater percentage of revenue on marketing, but there isn't an exact science for figuring out the right number. The key is to figure out which projects get you the return on investment you're seeking and to be very clear on how many starts you can manage at any given time. Remember, most builders don't need 10 to 20 leads per month, but just a handful of great sales-qualified leads per month that they receive on a consistent basis.

## THE BASICS

There are marketing strategies that everyone in the industry should be executing well. You can (and should) pick ways to go beyond this, but it's important to understand what the bare minimum looks like so you can do an audit and see where your business stands. As Vince Lombardi always said, "Get brilliant on the basics."

Some of the items on this list surprise our coaching clients because they've never considered them to be marketing. But the reality is whatever exposure people have with your business affects whether they want to raise their hand and pursue learning more about you—and potentially work with you.

1.  **Website**: This is your digital storefront, and you want it to pass the test with your customers and prospects.

Website design varies greatly, ranging from simple one-page sites to robust ones that have many features. There isn't one right answer for how complex your site should be, but it does need to be modern. We recommend always considering your website to be a work in progress. That way, you get into the habit of updating it on a regular basis, rather than going for several years without keeping it fresh. Make sure your home page is appealing and clear. To build trust, post good, professional photos of your people and projects. Include multiple ways to connect with you, such as phone, email, text, an online form, and social media.

2. **Search engine optimization (SEO):** You can sink a lot of money into SEO for various keywords, but the bare minimum is to get your website to pop up in the first page of search engine results without having to scroll when people search your company's name.

3. **Online reviews:** Customers rely on online reviews more than ever, especially for construction and trade businesses. If you don't actively manage this aspect of marketing, it's hurting your business. Ask your clients for an online review at the completion of their job—but only if they feel you have earned it. A lot of business owners only respond to the bad reviews, but that's a big mistake. People who write good reviews are even more likely to sing your praises if you show your appreciation for their support. Make sure you respond to all reviews online—whether good, bad, or indifferent. You don't want people to think you are only responding to the "squeaky wheels" and neglecting your raving fans. If you do get a bad review, don't sweat it. It isn't the end of the world. Just focus on getting some of your raving fans to leave good reviews. That will dilute the weaker ones.

4. **Signage:** One of the easiest marketing opportunities is having great-looking signage on vehicles and jobsites. Including your contact information is a best practice.

Also, have a variety of sign sizes in your inventory, and post the largest one you can on a jobsite.

5. **Branded uniforms**: When you and your team members are on the job, you want to look professional. Even if the customer you're working for isn't going to be there, you never know who else you'll run into in the neighborhood. Get branded T-shirts, golf shirts, or hats so everyone has a single, cohesive look.

6. **Door hangers**: When you work at a new site, leave door hangers at the neighbors' houses. If you're doing construction or a project that might be disruptive, a "pardon our dust" note can go a long way in building rapport. Don't be afraid to knock on doors to share this message in person, and hand the door hangers to people directly.

7. **Jobsite presence**: When you have your company's signage proudly posted at your jobsites, it's especially important to keep your work areas clean and organized. Make sure your team members aren't leaving cigarette butts in the street, empty water bottles in plain sight, or garbage scattered on the property. Don't play loud music while you're working, and be respectful of the neighbors.

8. **One-sheeter**: Create a simple, one-page document about your company. Include your services, differentiating factors, and contact info. Print it out on nice, heavy paper and keep it with you so you can hand it to prospects you meet.

9. **Vehicles**: A car wash can go a long way in giving off the impression that your team is organized and professional. Also remember to be an extra courteous driver when your company's name is printed on the vehicle.

The aforementioned list of must-haves should be part of your ongoing marketing efforts. Get into a rhythm where the tasks become so routine that you hardly have to think about them.

Once you have a good handle on the basics, you can elevate your marketing to the next level.

## NEXT LEVEL

Although there are hundreds—if not thousands—of unique marketing strategies you could employ for your business, our best advice is to start small and be conservative so that you can figure out what really moves the needle for you. Most companies in our industry only need three to four solid marketing strategies. That's it! You don't need to open Pandora's marketing box to be successful. It's much better to do a few strategies well than to do a lot in a mediocre way.

1. **Referrals:** Our company has worked with hundreds of businesses over the years, and we can tell you beyond a shadow of a doubt that referrals are the most impactful marketing initiative you can employ in this industry. A recommendation goes a long way, whether it's for a plumber, electrician, or custom home builder. You want your customers primed and ready to share your name with their friends and family. Luckily, there are a few strategies that make this process much easier:

   ❖ Set the stage at the beginning of new projects by saying up front that if you do a great job, you would be grateful if they would recommend you to their friends and family.

   ❖ Circle back at the end of the project to remind people that referrals are always appreciated. The best moment to do this is when customers are wowed. For custom home builders, this is when you hand over the keys and give them a welcome-home gift basket or something similar. It's important to note that there is a caveat here. When a client was difficult to work with or they weren't really in your target market, it doesn't make as much sense to ask for referrals. For best results, just focus on your grade-A clients for this marketing strategy. Remember, when you ask for a referral from a customer or client, you will most likely get referred to someone very similar to them.

❖ You shouldn't pay for referrals. You want them to refer you because of the outstanding job you've done for them, not because you're offering them a few dollars. It's smart to use your budget to thank clients for their support. Gift them a night at a nice hotel or send a surprise gift you know they'll love.

2. **Testimonials**: Along the same lines as referrals, testimonials increase trust. They show you've done an excellent job, and that people are thrilled with your work. Every time you have a happy customer, you should try to get a testimonial. You can follow the same practice as with referrals to tell clients up front that you would appreciate a testimonial if you do a good job, and follow up when the project closes out to remind them. To really use testimonials to your advantage, you should market the ones that relate to the type of work you want to do more of in the future. These testimonials can be written or video, and a mix of both can be extremely effective.

3. **Company newsletter**: Staying top of mind is key for converting leads and continuing to get referrals from past clients. A regular newsletter is a great way to do this. Some companies prefer to send a physical letter in the mail, and others choose to go digital. There are pluses and minuses to both approaches. You need to find what makes sense for your budget, your customers, and what you can realistically maintain long term.

4. **Lead magnets and funnels**: Here's where email marketing shines. When you offer something of value for free, you can entice people to visit your website and give you their email address. This enables you to keep them in your ecosystem and easily market to them in the future. We recommend creating a simple guide or

cheat sheet for solving common problems that visitors to your website can download. Choose a topic that people just visiting your site will find compelling. For example:

❖ Five ways to . . .
❖ Four mistakes people make when . . .
❖ Simple ways to save time and money on . . .

You can post this information as a PDF behind a sign-up form that's linked to your email marketing platform. That way, when people opt in to get the information, they are automatically added to your email list. You would be amazed at how effective this can be, especially when you share the lead magnet using social media, your website, or online ads.

5. **Strategic alliance program:** Go out of your way to develop relationships with a couple of businesses that have the same target market as you but sell a different product or service. For example, you might get to know architects, realtors, mortgage brokers, or interior designers. Find people you like and collaborate with them to refer one another's business. This shouldn't be a paid engagement because you don't want it to become a commodity.

6. **Advertising:** This can be a great way to build awareness in your business, but you need to make sure you're reaching the right target market. Social media advertising has become remarkably sophisticated, and it's easy to test a variety of messages and target demographics to see what works. You can also run remarketing ads where you specifically target people who have visited your website. Just be aware that ads are not always a good strategy for bringing in immediate leads, unless you're trying to get attention for a specific event, such as an open house or parade of homes. It's better to think of ads as a long-game tool for building awareness.

7. **Social media:** You don't need to be on every platform, but you should have a presence on one or two, and do it well. Think about where your customers hang out online and try focusing your efforts there. You should also consider which platforms work the best in terms of how you want to share information. If you're great at shooting and editing videos, TikTok or Instagram might be your best choice. If you like to share facts about your industry, Twitter might be best. (Some of our clients have used Twitter to continually get attention from reporters who were looking for industry experts. The articles they have been quoted in helped them reach a larger audience.)

As you decide where to focus your energy, I highly recommend filling out a simple one-page marketing plan. (Check out our strategic plan template online, which includes marketing: drilldownlevelup.com/resources.) If you're working with an SBGP coach, we have a template you can use to help you stay focused and organized. When you put your chosen strategies on paper, it becomes much easier to keep your colleagues in the loop and hold yourself accountable for following through with your marketing goals and strategies.

## ADJUST YOUR MESSAGING

If you're putting in consistent work with marketing but aren't getting enough leads or the kinds of leads you want, you might have an issue with your messaging. Marketing efforts can easily fall flat if the content isn't quite right. Unfortunately, this can be a confusing problem for business owners in any industry. It's hard to take a step back and see your company through the eyes of the people in your target market. What's most important for them to know about you? What would really set you apart, make you memorable, and help you win their business? We talked about this earlier in this chapter, and now would be a good time to go back and think about what you came up with. You might find that the language on your website and marketing materials doesn't capture the essence of your brand and points of difference.

We worked with a landscaping and hardscaping company that recently went through this process. The owner and his team loved putting in fireplaces, patios, walls, and fountains, so they wanted to focus on designing large outdoor living areas. But everyone was frustrated because most of their business was mowing small lawns for $50 a pop. The margin was so low that the company had to do a ton of jobs just to break even. This was problematic because the need for marketing increased, and they had to hire and manage more people. On top of that, employees weren't very engaged in their jobs because their passion didn't lie in mowing lawns. They wanted to do the more interesting and mentally challenging work of designing and building outdoor living areas.

Our team sat down with the owner and talked about how the business had gone in an undesirable direction, and how we could bring it back to the right path through focused marketing. We knew that if the company were going to get more big-ticket hardscaping jobs, it needed to build up its expertise in that niche.

"We do have some decent experience," the owner said. He pulled up photos on his phone and showed them to our team. Our jaws almost hit the floor. They had created many impressive outdoor spaces for both homes and businesses. We found ourselves practically screaming, "Why don't you have these pictures on your website?!" That's when the light bulb went off that the company did have a deep level of experience in custom hardscaping; they just weren't communicating it properly. Every picture on their website showed lawns, and not a single hardscape project.

That week, we had a professional photographer stop by all of their biggest hardscaping clients to take photos for the website and social media. They also got testimonials from those clients that talked specifically about the project details—none of which included mowing lawns. Finally, the company updated its website to focus more on high-end hardscaping work. They got more comfortable turning down leads that were too small to help them reach their goals, as well as owning the reality that they are not the cheapest option in the area.

Two years later, the company continues to experience consistent growth doing the kind of work they want most. It's no longer feast or famine with leads coming in, and they don't feel like they have to take small one-off jobs just to keep the lights on. They are now getting so many leads that they are able to be very particular on whom they wish to work with, thereby increasing their margins and team morale.

This is the power of adjusting your messaging.

In chapter 2, we covered your vision, goals, and strategy. We talked about the importance of being able to communicate your value to the right target market and hone in on your niche. This is where that hard work comes into play the most. When your messaging properly represents your business, your marketing is going to attract the kind of clients you want to work with.

Here are a few key points to consider when reflecting on your marketing message:

❖ **One-liner:** In one sentence, do you clearly describe the value you provide? Instead of having a broad message that you do all kinds of work, it's almost always more effective to niche down.

❖ **Three differentiators:** Are you clear on the factors that set you apart from your competition and make you unique? Make sure this is communicated on your website and marketing materials.

❖ **Branding:** Is your company's overall look appealing? Do the colors align with the brand personality? Are the graphics impressive, or do they look dated? Try to consider the aesthetics of your branding as though you've never seen them before. Most of the companies we've worked with have needed a bit of a refresher in this department.

A lot of business owners think through their messaging when they launch their business, but they don't always realize when they've outgrown their current content. The messaging you created for your business years ago might not be the right representation of who you are today. It's important to check in and evaluate your content on an ongoing basis as your business evolves and grows.

## MASTER RHYTHM AND CONSISTENCY

It's hard to throw the ball and catch it too. Yet, that's what we see most of our clients trying to do when it comes to marketing. Some businesses are big enough that it makes sense to employ a dedicated marketing person, but most companies have people who work in other roles help out with marketing in their spare time. This can be an economical option, and it might also be a good fit for team members who enjoy marketing. After all, some of the strategies we highlighted above are easy—and dare we say, fun! Marketing can be a creative outlet that's rewarding and different from other aspects of the business—and if you and your colleagues are enthusiastic about pitching in, that's great.

Unfortunately, the problem is that almost all marketing projects can easily get pushed to the back burner without any immediate consequences. If you forget to ask for a referral or to send a monthly newsletter, your business will not come crashing to the ground. So when work gets busy and you have an influx of projects, marketing could be the first thing you go without. And you might not be stressed about it because you have so much business coming in that scaling back on marketing seems totally fine—maybe even smart.

This kind of roller-coaster scenario puts you in a bad spot. When you get lax on consistent marketing, you're likely to feel it months later. And that might be around the time when projects start slowing down and you need more leads coming in. Suddenly, there's a scramble to catch up on everything that paused during the busy period, which is disruptive to other aspects of the company.

You need to get into a rhythm where you stay on top of marketing no matter what else is happening in the business. This work includes maintaining strategies listed earlier in this chapter under The Basics, as well as the three to four next-level strategies you choose to focus on.

Also keep in mind that some marketing strategies build awareness in your brand slowly rather than driving immediate leads. For example, you wouldn't expect to get a bunch of phone calls the day you put a new vehicle wrap on your company's truck. But if people in your community get to know your company through a variety of touchpoints, that awareness can ultimately lead to a phone call after weeks, months, or even years. That's why it's important to be consistent and keep up with marketing on an ongoing basis.

## HOW TO MEASURE RESULTS

There are simple things you can do to track where leads are coming in, such as a basic spreadsheet, installing Google Analytics on your website, using "bit.ly" links on social media, and asking people how they heard about you. However, marketing can be notoriously hard to measure, and it's nearly impossible to have a perfect system for tracking results. One reason for this is it's often more than one strategy that turns someone into a prospect. Maybe they drove past a yard sign every day for months on their way to work. Or they heard a friend mention your name a year ago, and it rang a bell when they did an online search for local builders. Or they visited your website a month ago, and you got their attention with an ad on Facebook. You won't always know the exact factors that contributed to bringing in specific leads, and that's OK. But it's important to do your best when it comes to tracking and measuring results so that you know what's worth your time moving forward.

Without consistency, there are too many moving parts to accurately assess your progress. But when you get into a rhythm, you give yourself a fair shot at determining what's actually working. After you master the basics, give yourself at least three months (one quarter) to set a baseline with any new marketing strategy. Assess how much time and money it took to implement, and the number of sales-qualified leads it brings in. This is how you set your priorities, troubleshoot, and refine your efforts.

Remember that marketing is a journey that takes time and patience, but it's something that anyone can get better at with a little practice and intentionality. Also, if you don't do something consistently, it's extremely hard to perfect it. Stay focused, and don't forget to have a little fun along the way.

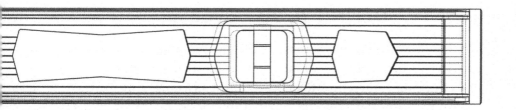

# CHAPTER 9

## SALES

P eople who have never worked in sales tend to have an oversimplified view of what it takes to get the job done. *You just talk to people and they either become customers or not, right?* For those of us who rely on sales to make a living, we know how much more complex the job is.

There are so many individual aspects to master, and if one thing is off, it creates ripples across the whole sales process and business as a whole. That's why sales can be elusive for many companies. It's difficult to pinpoint what's working, and what's not. And if you go about the process a little differently each time, it becomes nearly impossible to get an accurate read on your success.

This chapter is one of my favorites because sales is such a crucial part of every company, and almost all of the coaching clients we have worked with have been able to make major improvements to this aspect of their business. Even leaders who thought sales wasn't the thing that was holding them back from growing and improving their business have seen how transformative a few key changes can be in taking things to the next level.

# DEFINE YOUR PROCESS

Most builders and contractors are deeply involved in the sales process at their company. Founders typically start out selling, and over time, learn how to do it well. But as a company grows, they have less and less time to devote to sales—whether it's selling directly to clients or holding salespeople's hands. Being entrenched in the sales process often becomes one of the biggest roadblocks to growth.

About 10 years ago, I started working with David Belman of Belman Homes. It was a family business, and David had stepped into the key role of selling homes soon after he'd graduated high school. At that point, he had very little sales experience, and the company lacked a well-defined sales process. David learned mostly through trial and error, and over the years, he became highly skilled at selling. The problem was that he didn't want to spend all of his time selling, since he was also trying to manage the rest of the business. He hired a couple of salespeople, but everyone he hired was frustrated that they weren't reaching David's level of results.

My team frequently works with leaders who find themselves in a predicament like David's. We know, firsthand, how tough this problem can be. Luckily, we have developed proven strategies that help businesses refine and streamline their sales to make it easy for owners to define their process and hand off the baton to allow their salespeople to replicate their results.

With David, the first thing we did was write down all of the details of his sales process. We captured the nitty-gritty behind the ins and outs of Belman Homes. Up until that point, the vast majority of those important details had only been living in David's head. That made it incredibly laborious to train people because David essentially had to do a personalized brain dump into every single new salesperson he hired. And since the process wasn't written down, he found himself explaining the same thing to people more than once whenever they couldn't remember all of the details.

We helped David create a new system that ultimately transformed both his sales department and his business overall. We started by developing training materials for salespeople that allowed David to share the most salient points of his sales pitch in an easy-to-follow guide. He brainstormed all the questions and objections he was used to getting from prospects and wrote down the best way to respond to each one. He also created sales collateral to share with prospects so they would know what to expect from the sales process itself.

Once the new system was implemented, it was like night and day at Belman Homes. David no longer had to be involved in every sale to help it close. He could rely on his salespeople to get the job done right, just as they had been trained to do. The company's conversion rate increased dramatically, and David finally had the time to focus on other areas of the business.

Defining the sales process was a game changer because it unlocked the power of consistency. You need to run the sales process the exact same way every single time so that you develop uniformity in what you're doing—and to get consistent results. This enables you to record your process and train other team members to do the job as well as you do—or even better.

You might be thinking, "Sure, consistency sounds great in theory, but it's hard to run a prospect through a sales process the exact same way every time. Each prospect has different questions and needs, and we tailor the messaging to meet the person." I understand where you're coming from, and I agree that in certain ways you need to meet prospects where they are when you communicate. This can make it harder to develop a consistent process and train your salespeople. However, there's a trick to maintaining consistency in your sales meetings that often gets overlooked. Remember, a great sales process is nothing more than a consistent way to gather, store, and share information with your prospect and distribute that information with your team.

## DON'T LET YOUR PROSPECT TAKE THE LEAD

In every sales meeting with a prospective client, someone will take the lead. It will either be you or the prospect. When prospects lead sales conversations, you tend to get subpar outcomes. You've probably experienced this before and know how frustrating it can be. If a prospect takes control, it can throw you off balance and cause you to backpedal into a reactive mode. You get peppered with rapid-fire questions and find yourself talking about random aspects of your company that you weren't planning on discussing. This flow of information doesn't paint the best picture of how you work or why you're the best builder for the job.

What a lot of people don't know is that you can take control of prospect sales meetings simply by telling them that you will do so. A best practice is to inform prospects from the onset that you have a specific process from start to finish, and it starts with the very first meeting. This might feel pushy, but customers actually prefer for you to take the lead in this kind of situation since they are coming to you as the expert. When someone throws you off your normal message, you can easily jump back into the script because you've already teed up that you have a set process for doing things in your company. For instance, simply saying, "As I mentioned earlier, we've been in this business for X years, and we have developed a really great process from start to finish. I usually address this kind of question later because of X. At this point, what's most important is going over Y, before I address your concerns."

This allows you and your salespeople to lead meetings consistently and deliver the same message with authority every time. Your goal should be to make this process so routine that you hardly even have to think about it. In fact, if it becomes boring and you feel like a broken record, that's how you know you're doing it right. Personally, I've gotten so comfortable talking with SBGP prospects that meetings with a prospective coaching client are a breeze. Sales should be rote repetition and muscle memory.

Once you have this level of consistency, you can level up your messaging, making small tweaks to better connect with individual prospects. For example, you can use DISC to better relate and build rapport, but you really need to have a solid baseline with your process before you can successfully tailor your message to individual prospects.

## PRESENT LIKE A PROFESSIONAL

I would be remiss if I didn't touch on the importance of professionalism in making a good impression. In this industry, you're often asking someone to make one of the biggest purchases of their life. When you provide a sales proposal, it should feel like there was considerable time and care put into it so that the prospect feels like they are getting a lot of value for the price.

First and foremost, you will not be successful sending sales proposals for expensive projects over email. People usually skip ahead in a document to look at the price, and they may not go back to read anything else. If you offer incredible value that sets you apart from your competitors and justifies your price, there's a good chance that will go right over your client's head if you don't walk them through your quote in person. If they absolutely can't meet in person, schedule a video conference so that you can still connect face-to-face, and you can quickly answer any questions.

When meeting with a prospect or client, dress to impress. Showing up in dirty jobsite clothes or an unwashed vehicle looks unprofessional. The same mentality holds true for the sales materials you provide. When proposals look nice, it shows that you are willing to go the extra mile. Don't give prospects something that looks like you slapped it together at the last minute in your basement. All sales materials should be printed in color on your company letterhead and include images or infographics and be neatly organized in a nice folder. Also, opt for heavy weight paper; 24-pound paper is my favorite. Details matter.

## FOLLOW UP PROPERLY

In addition to building consistency within your prospect sales meetings, you must have a strong follow-up system. My team and I recently worked with a roofing business that found this out firsthand. The company was still struggling to be profitable after 10 years in business. The owner thought they had a marketing problem where they weren't getting enough good leads, but we had a hunch that wasn't the real issue.

We analyzed what was going on behind the scenes and realized they were losing about half of their prospects because they didn't have an organized follow-up system. They'd get leads but fail to respond to them in a timely manner, so prospects would naturally take their business elsewhere. When work was busy and they were up to their ears in roofing jobs, they hardly noticed they were flaking out on potential projects. Unfortunately, they were missing out on an easy way to scale the business. This wasn't a problem with marketing; it was a problem with their sales process.

We coached the owner through establishing a follow-up process for the sales team where they respond to all new leads within 48 hours. They also implemented a CRM system to help track past leads that haven't closed yet and circle back with them at an appropriate time. That's all it took for them to transform their profitability. As a result, they are on track for their best year after a decade in business.

Most of the builders and trade companies we work with have an opportunity to improve their follow-up process. One of the most efficient ways to make sure that leads aren't falling through the cracks is to utilize CRM, but a lot of small businesses do just fine tracking leads in a spreadsheet. The important thing is getting into a rhythm where someone on your team checks in with leads on a regular basis—no matter how busy things get.

## UNDERSTAND SALES GOALS AND CONVERSION RATES

Sales is a numbers game. To win the game, you need enough qualified leads coming in, and a high enough conversion rate to make a profit. To analyze how your business is doing, we highly recommend using a scorecard to track your numbers. The following image shows an example of how a home builder and a roofer might track their sales.

## EXAMPLE SCORECARD

### Custom Home Builder
### Monthly Sales Goals

| | Qualified Prospects | Conversion Rate | Meetings with Prospects | Conversion Rate | Proposals Presented | Conversion Rate | Contracts Signed | Booked Revenue |
|---|---|---|---|---|---|---|---|---|
| Goal | 8 | 50% | 4 | 50% | 2 | 50% | 1 | $500,000 |
| Month 1 | 6 | 83% | 5 | 60% | 3 | 33% | 1 | $560,000 |
| Month 2 | 8 | 38% | 3 | 33% | 1 | 100% | 1 | $520,000 |

### Roofing Contractor
### Monthly Sales Goals

| | Qualified Prospects | Conversion Rate | Meetings with Prospects | Conversion Rate | Proposals Presented | Conversion Rate | Contracts Signed | Booked Revenue |
|---|---|---|---|---|---|---|---|---|
| Goal | 40 | 50% | 20 | 50% | 10 | 50% | 5 | $100,000 |
| Month 1 | 25 | 20% | 5 | 60% | 3 | 100% | 3 | $45,000 |
| Month 2 | 35 | 34% | 12 | 83% | 10 | 80% | 8 | $150,000 |

Each of these columns is important because it provides data on a step in the sales process. Depending on what the numbers look like, you can begin to identify what's working and what has room for improvement.

As an example, a lot of builders and contractors want to close as many leads as possible and are surprised when we tell them that's not a good goal. A healthy conversion rate is a lot lower than what people tend to expect. For instance, we've had clients who were happy with their 80 to 90 percent conversion rate on their scorecard. But having that much success closing shows that there is a problem: They aren't charging enough. Think about it. If everyone wants to buy what you're selling, you should raise your prices.

Converting 50 percent of leads is a good baseline, but it should be near the top of your sales bell curve. Most successful builders close at least 30 percent of their leads. If you're around 30 percent or lower, you either have a problem with your sales process (as discussed earlier in this chapter), or you're wasting time on unqualified leads.

Just to make sure we're on the same page, a *sales-qualified lead* is someone in your target market with the wherewithal to buy from you and who is going to buy from either you or your competition. An unqualified lead is the opposite. The challenge is properly qualifying leads before you invest your precious time in trying to sell to them.

Almost all of our coaching clients have this issue when we start working together. Salespeople spend a lot of time with prospects, and they get frustrated when a big chunk of those leads doesn't convert. If that happens to you, you need to improve your vetting process and become more selective about whom you choose to engage and work with.

A great way to weed out leads that are less likely to close is to have a professional service agreement (PSA). This is a detailed quote that prospects pay you to create because it takes you time and effort to assess their needs. PSAs work well if you're selling custom solutions at a significant price point, such as a new home design, a remodeling project, or a hardscaped patio. You can do the initial part of the estimate for free and provide prospects with a preliminary ballpark figure, but when it turns into work beyond that to nail down a price, don't be afraid to charge.

We always tell clients that if prospects aren't willing to pay for a detailed estimate, they aren't a strong enough lead to pursue. You are not running a bidding mill. You can't give it all away for free, because it's an enormous waste of time and doing so would make it easy for prospects to use your hard work and shop it around to get a lower price.

When prospects aren't willing to pay for a PSA in return for your time, then feel confident that you don't want their business anyway. Pick your customer base like a baseball manger picks his team. You only have so many people you can put on the field. You're either going to have an all-star team or a minor league squad. With a team full of ideal customers, you will have better margins, and your team will be happy because they are dealing with great people.

Remember, the magic number for closing is typically less than 50 percent. That means you *want* half of your prospects to drop out of the sales process. Ted Williams is lauded as one of the greatest Hall of Fame baseball players of all time. At his best, his batting average was .400—meaning he only got a hit 40 percent of the time. But in baseball, that's essentially perfect. I like to keep that in mind when I'm analyzing sales numbers because it reminds me that 100 percent is not my target.

One of our clients who mastered the art of the conversion rate is an 81-year-old builder in Texas. He has an incredible conversion rate because he has perfected his company's simple sales process. Each qualified prospect has a scorecard that his salespeople fill out by ranking them on a scale of 1 to 10. The owner keeps a copy of each scorecard when a prospect signs a contract. He personally fills it out based on how good of a client they are, and then he goes back and sees the number they were given initially by his employee. Based on his experience, he has cross-referenced enough rankings to know exactly how high a qualified lead needs to score in order to pursue a relationship with the prospect. It's not a Jedi mind trick; lead scoring is just simple math.

## SETTING GOALS

Most business owners have some level of sales goals, but we also talk with a lot of clients who operate under vague metrics. You really need to know what your end goal is for each week, month, quarter, and year. While every company will differ in terms of the metrics they use to determine that, you must have a system of measurement in place. You can choose to quantify this by the ideal number of projects you want in a year or the number of projects that would bring you to your max capacity. Another approach that works for some builders and contractors is to start with revenue and then backtrack to figure out the number of projects you need to take on from there to meet those goals.

No matter what you use as your benchmark, knowing your sales goals empowers your team to hit that number. Going back to our earlier conversation in chapter 3 about knowing your numbers, it's absolutely vital that everyone on your sales team knows what success looks like. Keep in mind that sales is an iterative process. A good method for making these incremental improvements is to track your sales using scorecards.

One way to create effective and accurate sales metrics is to reverse engineer it. For example, if your goal is to build four homes, then how many proposals must you create to get four new contracts? To get that many proposals, how many client meetings must you have? To get that many client meetings, how many qualified leads will you need?

## COMPENSATING SALES TEAMS

As an owner, your goal should be to make sure the business can run without you being involved in the day to day. One of the most important positions that will enable you to take a step back is having a talented salesperson. To attract and retain people who are truly excellent at their job, you'll need to offer strong financial incentives. Full commission seems like it would be ideal for you, the employer, but it isn't a good recipe for creating longstanding team members. The best practice is giving salespeople a base salary with commission. Obviously, you're taking on some risk paying a base salary; if sales aren't made, you're out thousands of dollars. But remember that your salespeople are also taking a risk accepting a job that doesn't guarantee the full amount they want to make. Both parties take on risk, so therefore both are highly motivated to work together and drive sales. The tricky part is structuring the base pay and commission such that the numbers work for everyone.

There are a few ways to go about this, but we recommend paying a base salary that is half of the expected total. If fair compensation for a successful person in this role is $100,000, $50,000 would come from salary and $50,000 would be expected from sales. If you want your salespeople to sell five houses per year, you would offer $10,000 for each house sold.

That said, you need to look more closely at your numbers to make sure this would still enable you to earn a predetermined profit on your projects. (That's why we covered the basics on profitability in chapter 3. Refer back to your numbers if you need a refresher.)

Total compensation on sales shouldn't exceed 19 to 20 percent of gross margin for a given project. As an example, if your gross profit on a $600,000 house is 15 percent, you would make $90,000. No more than 20 percent of that ($18,000) should go to the salesperson. When paying a base salary, some of this is already accounted for in overhead. So 50 percent of the $18,000 is baked into salary, and 50 percent is the commission per sale, which would be $9,000. If a salesperson sells five houses per year, their total combined salary and commission would be $90,000.

To make it clear to everyone, you should put together a plan that shows how much salespeople will make if they sell *below, at,* or *more* than expected. The upper limit is the capacity of the company to provide the services, which needs to be clear so that salespeople don't sell more than you can realistically deliver.

It's important to note that it isn't just the amount that matters when it comes to compensation. The timing is also important. You should pay a decent portion of bonus compensation, such as 50 percent, right after a sale closes. This gives salespeople instant gratification and motivates them to sell more. Structure your payment plan to make sure that they get money along the way while also keeping it simple for administrative purposes.

Many builders and contractors also incentivize sales through a bonus program. Once people meet their sales goal for the year, anything above that is rewarded with a higher commission. Since the company will make more money on those sales than on other sales because the overhead is already covered, it won't hurt profits to pay a little more for commission.

Sometimes a bonus structure is the best solution. We had a client, Smith Family HVAC, that wanted to have add-on service contracts added to their sales offerings. However, they were relying on the field technician (with no sales experience) to sell it directly to customers while on the jobsite.

Since this was out of the field technician's comfort zone, we advised the business owner to create a bonus structure, which made it fun. They put people into teams, and whoever sold the least had to cook the winning team lunch. Getting creative with their approach brought their staff together and boosted company morale. As a result, today, they get more of the type of sales that they want.

## Compensation Plan Template

Name: _____

Territory: _____

**Responsibilities:**

1. Meet sales goals
2. Keep sales management system up to date
3. Communicate effectively with prospects

**Base Compensation: $_____ per month ($_____ annually)**

**Sales Goals:**

Annual Sales Goal = $_____

Q1 Sales Goal = $_____ (___percent of total Quota)

Q2 Sales Goal = $_____ (___percent of total Quota)

Q3 Sales Goal = $_____ (___percent of total Quota)

Q4 Sales Goal = $_____ (___percent of total Quota)

**1. Sales Commission:**

- ___ percent of expected gross margin

**Projected Total Compensation:**

| @ 80 percent of Target Plan | @ 100 percent of Target Plan | @ 120 percent of Target Plan |
|---|---|---|
| Annual = $_____ | Annual = $_____ | Annual = $_____ |
| Q1 = $_____ | Q1 = $_____ | Q1 = $_____ |
| Q2 = $_____ | Q2 = $_____ | Q2 = $_____ |
| Q3 = $_____ | Q3 = $_____ | Q3 = $_____ |
| Q4 = $_____ | Q4 = $_____ | Q4 = $_____ |

Just like anything else in life, practice makes perfect. The more you practice these sales principles to iron out the kinks and achieve consistency, the better results you and your team will get. It won't be perfect overnight. You will need to continuously evaluate your progress and adjust until you have a system that works for your company. But I promise that when you level up your ability to efficiently and consistently close qualified leads, you will unlock a new level of growth.

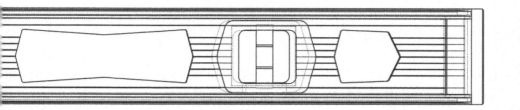

# CHAPTER 10

## TAKING CARE OF CUSTOMERS

When the Green Bay Packers rush out of the tunnel before a game at Lambeau Field, the stands erupt with thunderous applause. If you aren't expecting it, it's startling enough to make you spill your *root beer*. An electric sense of hope fills the stadium at the start of every game, even during losing seasons. The fans cheer because they believe that today the home team will taste victory. Teams win or lose, but true fans—the type that paint their stomachs green and gold—are loyal to the team no matter what. This loyalty is built on trust. The Green Bay Packers have some of the most loyal, raving fans in the league. Why? One major reason is they have won 13 NFL championships. But it's not just about winning, it's also about giving the fans what they really want: the chance to feel connected to something bigger than themselves.

You can learn a lot about customer satisfaction from watching Green Bay Packers' home games on TV. Inside the heart of every loyal fan is the belief that whoever they root for will take care of them. Whether that's you or your competitor depends on how willing you are to go the extra mile in your communication to let them know that you care about them as a person first, and as a customer second.

As a small business, taking care of your customers is about letting them know they can trust you no matter what. Your customer relationships are the oxygen line of your business; without them, you won't survive. But keeping customers happy can be a challenge, unless you have a solid plan in place. One of the best approaches that we've found to maintain an ongoing, steady stream of business is to raise the bar on customer service and give them a fantastic experience. The goal is to transform them from just another average paying customer to a raving fan.

Raving fans are the customers who love your business, your employees, and, most importantly, the results from your company. Without ever being prompted, they pass on your company's information to friends, family, and even total strangers. They are so satisfied with the quality of your service that they are virtually unpaid members of your sales team.

Regular satisfied customers may be happy with your product, but they likely aren't telling anyone about it. Raving fans, on the other hand, can't help but go the extra mile to support your business. That's the difference. When you have raving fans, you don't need as many leads, because they will help bring you new business.

Now, you may think that this sounds too good to be true. After all, how on earth can you get people practically bubbling over about your building company or trade business? Even though your company isn't as exciting as your favorite sports team, and probably no one will paint their chest or face with your logo, the concept of keeping customers happy is the same. If you perform your job well, and have the track record to prove it, people will support you. The Green Bay Packers have tons of fans who believe in them, and they have the Super Bowl hardware to back it up. But they also give their raving fans something extra.

Raving fans crave connection above all else. When you

establish a genuine connection with your customers, it instills in them a sense of community. And when people feel connected to a network of other people, it naturally creates trust. While you should always strive for a high standard of excellence, transforming customers into raving fans isn't just about the quality of your work. What's more important is the quality *of your connection with your customers.* In a tight-knit industry that focuses on helping families, you'd be surprised how excited people get to share their experiences about working with a trustworthy company that went the extra mile to establish a connection with them. It may not happen overnight, but with a little practice and a lot of patience, it can happen for your construction or trade company.

## BUILDING RELATIONSHIPS

If you want to create raving fans, you have to put in a lot of work to build a relationship first. To make this happen, it has to be part of your process. Relationships take work, and most of the challenge comes in the form of learning how to consistently communicate with your customers. You can't just be accommodating in the beginning of the relationship. Once you make a great first impression, you have to continue to be attentive for the duration of the project, which could be many months. (Not to mention staying in touch when the job is finished.) That's why it's so important to make building relationships more than just an item on your to-do list; it needs to be part of your actual business plan.

For some lucky entrepreneurs, frequent communication comes naturally, but that isn't true for everyone. Managing current customers and past leads, as well as following up on new business and referrals, can feel like a full-time job. This is why you have to put together a system to keep you and your team accountable. This process doesn't have to be hard. It can be as simple as a spreadsheet that tells you when to follow up and what type of message you need to send on which day, and provides a basic template that you will follow to write your message. If you or your project managers don't have something like this in place, chances are you won't stay in contact with customers as closely as you should. Communication platforms such as CoConstruct and Buildertrend make it easy to send messages directly through the portal, streamlining all of your communication in one place to make it easier to manage.

One system that works well for larger projects is scheduling regular client check-in meetings. This gives clients a designated time to ask questions, which cuts back on other communications outside those meetings. It also provides your team with plenty of opportunity to get real-time feedback on how things are going. Don't be afraid to directly ask if customers are happy with the work or the process. This goes a long way toward showing that you care and helps address any issues before they turn into something bigger.

Feeling heard is one of the greatest building blocks to forming trust in a customer relationship. When you allow your customers to share what's on their mind, it creates a consistent customer feedback loop that allows you to take the appropriate action to guarantee their satisfaction.

After a project is completed, your regular communication can scale back, but it shouldn't end.

A lot of builders and trade companies wonder why they should try to develop ongoing relationships with their clients when the likelihood of them buying again is very low. What they don't realize is that happy clients will talk about them and give them referrals to family and friends. However, this tends to only work for a limited period of time, such as when a job was recently completed and it's fresh in the customer's mind. Someone might be a raving fan about their beautiful new deck for the first summer or two, but after that they probably won't talk about it as much, especially if they haven't heard anything from the company since the day it was finished. But when companies keep in touch with customers and continue relationships after the job is complete, the situation is totally different.

For example, we work with a builder in Michigan named

Greg Windemuller who really embraced staying in touch with his clients and went the extra mile to add a personal touch. He developed a system for sending small birthday gifts, holiday cards, and one-off messages asking how everyone was doing with the house. As a result, Greg's customers remembered him years later and still felt like they could trust him.

One day, Greg was checking in with a past customer who mentioned he had some lakefront property he was trying to sell. He told Greg that one of his relatives was going to build on it, but plans fell through and they were now looking for a realtor to sell the property. This was interesting news to Greg, who also happened to be a licensed realtor. Greg told his customer he would be happy to list the property for free, but if it sold, he wanted his firm to be the designated builder for the house. Fast-forward a year, and Greg's company is in the process of building a $1.5 million home on that property. This never would have happened if Greg hadn't made it a priority to stay in touch with past customers. In this industry, long-term relationships are the name of the game.

Now, you might be thinking that staying in touch with past customers sounds good in theory, but it could also open a can of worms. What if you call people you did work for a year ago and they tell you that something isn't quite right, or they want you to come out and fix an issue? Couldn't that turn into a lot of extra work?

Instead of viewing feedback from customers as a burden, we recommend looking at it as an opportunity. First of all, no company is perfect. Try as we might, things don't always go exactly how we plan. It's not fun to hear that a subcontractor did something incorrectly, materials didn't hold up like they should have, or an honest mistake was made somewhere along the line. But that's reality. It's better to be aware of those issues and have a chance to correct them than to avoid customer feedback altogether.

When customers tell you about simple problems, fixing them can actually be great opportunities to continue building relationships. Replacing a broken doorknob or touching up some paint shouldn't be a big deal. Obviously, you want to set boundaries so this doesn't turn into doing projects for free, but you want customers to feel like you're taking care of them.

Have a system in place to handle this kind of work without it derailing other projects. Instead of taking one of your carpenters off a job, develop relationships with a couple of trusted handymen who can be your go-to people. It may cost you $30 or $40 an hour, but if it turns a customer into a raving fan and leads to $700,000 referral, it's well worth it.

Here's where your marketing mindset really comes into play. If you do this sort of thing consistently, it will become part of your company's reputation. This type of premium customer service is what can become the difference maker between sitting around waiting for the phone to ring and having great leads consistently fall into your lap.

## CRITICAL NONESSENTIALS

Have you ever gone out to eat at a restaurant that you haven't been to in months, and the waiter remembers your favorite entrée? Or maybe they remember something you mentioned during a single conversation the last time you dined there, and they ask you about it? It doesn't happen often, but when this type of interaction happens, it makes you feel special.

Knowing the little things that your customers like makes them feel valued, and is a great way to create raving fans. At SBGP, we like to call these tidbits of information *critical non-essentials*. We capture these facts from our own clients using a new client questionnaire in our onboarding process. This is how we learn their birthdays, the names of their kids or pets, and fun facts such as their favorite hobbies and restaurants. This information helps us get to know our clients, and makes it easy for us to surprise them down the road with gifts we know they'll love.

Depending on your customer volume and average price point, a yearly birthday gift might be some of the cheapest marketing you can do. For example, if you build 10 homes a year and then send each of those clients a $20 birthday gift every year thereafter, you're only spending $200 over the course of 10 years to keep in touch and continue to delight each customer. Your chances of each of those relationships turning into at least one good referral over the course of those 10 years is quite high.

With just a $20 birthday gift, you can amaze your past customers by sending them things that align with their interests and hobbies and show how well you know them. For example, if your client does yoga, send a new yoga mat or a travel bag for a mat. These simple things don't cost a lot but mean a lot to the people you do business with. If you want to go the extra mile, add the names of your customer's family members inside the birthday card (e.g., I hope Pat and the kids are making you feel special today.) It doesn't take a lot of extra effort to pull out their questionnaire and write a few names down, but it does go a long way toward making people feel valued. This type of genuine connection is what will win you raving fans who will give you amazing referrals.

If you're a trade business owner who does higher volumes, such as a plumbing or HVAC company, don't skip out on client relationships just because you can't spend as much to keep in touch with each customer. A number of years back, we worked with a client who owns an HVAC company. Whenever his team does any kind of service work, he puts a sticker with his logo and contact info on each system, with an explanation of whom to call for what issue. He also collects customers' email addresses and sends them their "tips and tricks" quarterly newsletter. He has installed over 30,000 HVAC systems in the Portland area, and they all have his sticker on their HVAC units and every customer was opted in to his email newsletter. Today, he dominates the market, because anytime someone has a problem, he's the guy they call.

How do you go the extra mile? It's not the big things, it's the little details that form an emotional connection that win customers' hearts. To maintain successful relationships, you will want to also incorporate face-to-face connections in order to make lasting memories. Sometimes, going above and beyond means more than just a card in the mail. You can get creative by throwing parties or housewarming events for your customers. Whenever possible, you should find a reason to celebrate something, such as when our client, Classic Kitchens, threw a big party for their 20th anniversary. At the party, they offered raffles, free family photos, face painting, and even games for the kids. The event was a huge success, and it earned Classic Kitchens thousands of dollars in business from referrals. This was an easy way to get all of their past customers all in one place, swapping stories about their kitchens and getting a chance to meet and mingle with other like-minded community members.

For most of your customers, their family home is the most expensive purchase they'll ever make. Why not borrow a page from Classic Kitchens' playbook and use that as an excuse to celebrate and throw a housewarming party for them? By welcoming your customers to their new neighborhood, you'll make them feel more at home in the house you built for them. You can let them know that they hired the right builder by inviting their friends, neighbors, and family to come celebrate with them. When you and your team show up at their front door with a truck bed full of catered food that everyone loves, your company will win serious brownie points. People naturally coming up to your team to thank them for hosting such a wonderful event turns into an easy conversation that can generate new leads and warm referrals. (SBGP will award you bonus points if you and your team ditch the takeout and get behind the grill yourselves.)

Remember, developing a relationship is a lot like dancing. There's always a back and forth that requires rhythm and consistency. You can't just stick a card in the mail, and you can't always throw parties for your past customers year after year. You need to communicate in the right cadence, which means mixing in multiple forms of communication. Once you know what your customers like and you build a rapport with them, you can tailor your communication style to fit their personal needs. Finding a good rhythm gets easier over time. It just takes a little practice and experimentation to hit the nail on the head.

When you prioritize consistent communication, your customers will feel like their needs are always being met. If you make them feel valued often enough, they will naturally grow to become raving fans. The best way your company can ensure this happens is to go above and beyond to create a company culture that is memorable. People won't remember the names of the materials you sourced, or all the subcontractors you hired. They will remember the faces they met at a housewarming party or cookout, and how they connected with the members of your staff who signed their birthday card. Every time they send a new referral to do more business with you, they will think back to how well your team treated them. And when they get your holiday greeting card in the mail or receive your thoughtful gift, they won't think about how much it cost. Instead, what will stick in their mind is how great they felt when you helped make their house their dream home.

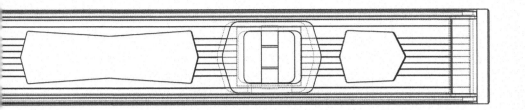

# CHAPTER 11

## LEVELING UP YOUR FINANCIAL PLANNING

Let's imagine you're headed out for work one morning. The sun is shining, and birds are singing, but as soon as you get inside your truck, something feels off. You look around but can't quite put your finger on what's different. You shrug it off as your coffee not having kicked in yet, but as you reverse down the driveway, you realize that your dashboard looks different. You rub your eyes. You must not have gotten enough sleep. You put the truck in drive and take a deep breath because it's looking like it's going to be an interesting day.

As you continue down your street, the sunrise makes such an incredible glare on your windshield that you can hardly see a thing. It almost looks like something greasy is coating the windshield. You go to flip on the windshield wipers, but nothing happens. Great. This is just what you need when you're running late. You were already wondering if you would need to stop and get gas—but wait, the gas gauge is bouncing up and down as if the sensor has gone haywire. That's when you notice the speedometer is doing the same thing. What in the world is going on?

You quickly pull over to the side of the road and roll down your window for some fresh air. You have to be at work in 15 minutes, but how could you possibly drive there with your truck in this condition? You can't see where you're going, know how fast you're going, or tell whether you have enough gas to get there.

If this strange situation truly happened to you, what would you do? Would you live on the wild side and try to drive your truck to the jobsite, or would you decide that being prudent made more sense? And what if this situation weren't just an anomaly, and instead, this is what your truck were like every day? These might sound like ridiculous questions. Who would choose to drive a vehicle they can't really see out of or trust to get them where they need to go safely?

It might sound crazy, but many business owners are in a similar situation with their financials. There are a variety of calculations that provide valuable information about the business, but many owners don't know how to run these numbers—or how to interpret the results. If you've never had these numbers, you probably don't realize how helpful they are for monitoring the health of the business, pinpointing financial issues, and making informed decisions. On the flip side, if you're used to having a lot of financial metrics and understand how to use them, not having access to this data is akin to driving a truck without a speedometer, gas gauge, or windshield wipers. Once you learn how to level up your financial planning, you will never want to go back.

When we start working with new clients, most of them have at least one subpar issue with their finances. Maybe cash flow is an issue, or their margins are low, or they aren't achieving the net profits they want. Additionally, very few of them know the exact numbers for how much they can afford in overhead, or when they can afford to hire a new employee and how much to pay them. Without this kind of knowledge, they're forced into a spot where they're making uninformed decisions. Let's be honest here. Every business owner has to

## REMINDER OF TERMS FROM CHAPTER 3:

❖ **cost of goods:** *the amount paid for materials and labor used to build or remodel a home*

❖ **expenses (also known as overhead):** *the costs of running a business, including rent, utilities, taxes, association fees, membership dues, office supplies, fuel, office staff, insurance, and marketing costs, and are unrelated to project costs*

❖ **gross profit:** *the difference between income and cost of goods*

❖ **gross profit margin (also known as gross profit percentage):** *financial gain expressed as a percentage of income (gross profit/income); not always shown in Quickbooks, but can be easily calculated.*

❖ **income:** *money or revenue coming into a business*

❖ **net ordinary income:** *the amount of money left over after cost of goods and expenses have been paid (income minus cost of goods minus expenses)*

❖ **net profit margin (also known as net profit percentage):** *net ordinary income expressed as a percentage of income (net ordinary income/income); not always shown in Quickbooks, but can be easily calculated*

make some decisions based on finances. But most of the time, they do it based on how much they have in their account right now. There are much better ways to get more-robust data and be more strategic.

In this chapter, we will cover the basic calculations you should be running on a regular basis. In chapter 3, we talked about the importance of having an accurate P&L statement, and you need to have that done to use the tools in this chapter. If you aren't a numbers person, that's OK. None of the tools or formulas you need to know are overly complicated. In fact, you probably did more-difficult calculations in your high school math classes. The trick is knowing how to interpret the data.

# UNDERSTAND LEAD INDICATORS VERSUS LAG INDICATORS

When we're interpreting data, the first thing to know is that financials aren't just numbers on paper. The numbers tell the story of a decision you made or didn't make. They are all reflective of your actions, or actions you didn't take.

Some numbers show what's likely to happen in the future, giving you options to make adjustments and change the outcomes. These lead indicators are like having a crystal ball for your business. If you know how much business you need this quarter and your conversion rates from leads to qualified leads to proposals to contracts, then you can work the numbers backward to calculate how many leads you need to meet your goal.

Other financial data, like the numbers on your P&L, are considered lag indicators, such as how much revenue you earned last quarter. By the time you know that number, it's history, and there's nothing you can do to change it. It's important to review your P&L on a monthly basis to assess how your numbers are fluctuating. You want to stay on top of this because as time passes, the data becomes less and less useful because it lags further and further behind.

## EXAMPLE: ABC HOME BUILDER

We're going to take you through some specific numbers as an example to show you how to use the data in your P&L. ABC Home Builder's key numbers are shown on the next page. In the sections that follow, we will reference this information to demonstrate how to do various calculations.

| Revenue | (A) | $1,000,000 | | | |
| Cost of Goods | (B) | $800,000 | 80.0% | (F) | COG % |
| Gross Profit | (C) | $200,000 | 20.0% | (G) | Gross Profit Margin |
| Expenses (Overhead) | (D) | $100,000 | | | |
| Net Ordinary Income | (E) | $100,000 | 10.0% | (H) | Net Profit Margin |

### Gross Profit

This number shows your profitability before deducting expenses.

- ❖ (A) - (B) = (C)
- ❖ Revenue - Cost of Goods = Gross Profit

Here's an example of what this looks like for ABC Home Builder:

- ❖ $1,000,000 - $800,000 = $200,000

Take a moment and calculate your gross profit from your P&L now and write it down.

My gross profit is: _____

Identifying this number is important not only for knowing your profitability, but because it is used in other calculations that shed even more light on your business.

### Gross Profit Margin

This number shows your profitability expressed as a percentage of income. Your P&L statement might have your gross profit percentage included, but not all accounting software has that. If it doesn't, you can easily calculate it yourself. Using your P&L, do the following calculation:

- ❖ G / A = GPM

Here's an example of what this looks like for ABC Home Builder:

❖ $200,000 / $1,000,000 = 20\%$

Take a moment to calculate your gross profit margin now and write it down.

My gross profit margin is: _____

## Breakeven Point

This is the amount of revenue your business will need to make to have all of your expenses paid for, with zero left over for profit. This number is important to know because it gives you a solid baseline for how much you need to make each month or quarter just to cover expenses. The calculation is very simple:

❖ D / G = Breakeven
❖ Expenses / Gross Profit Margin = Breakeven

Here's an example of what this looks like for ABC Home Builder:

❖ $100,000 / 20\% = \$500,000$

In other words, they would need to do $500,000 in business to breakeven. If homes are averaging $400,000, ABC Home Builder would need to build one to two homes to breakeven.

If your overhead expenses change, as they often do when a company is growing, your breakeven point will change. For example, if you wanted to add an additional office staff member who would have a salary of $50,000 a year, then your breakeven point would change:

❖ 9(D + $50,000) / Gross Profit percent = Additional Revenue Needed
❖ $150,000 / 20\% = \$750,000$

Some people think that if they have $50,000 more in expenses, they just need to do $50,000 more in business to cover them, but you can see that is not the case. (Not every dollar you bring in is profit.)

Take a moment to calculate what your breakeven point is now based on your P&L and write it down.

My breakeven point is: _____

Ask your SBGP coach about the handy Breakeven Template we

have to help you automatically calculate your breakeven point. The template will tell you exactly how much you need to make each month and for the year to break even. This becomes a very simple way to answer a lot of questions that come up about whether you should move forward with something for your business. If you're considering paying for a new marketing campaign, or moving to a bigger office, or upgrading the team's laptops, this calculation will help you understand how your breakeven point would change. It will also help you determine how you could adjust other numbers in your business, such as your gross profit margin and markup, to be able to afford additional expenses.

### Desired Net Profit Margin (Net Profit Percentage)

You will need to find another important number: your desired net profit margin. The net profit is the money that is left over after you've paid for cost of goods and expenses. For our SBGP clients, we shoot to get them to a healthy net profit margin of 8–12 percent of overall revenue.

- ❖ (D + Desired Net Profit) / G = Required Revenue
- ❖ (Overhead Expenses + Desired Net Profit) / Gross Profit Margin = Required Revenue

Here's what this looks like for ABC Home Builder:

- ❖ ($100,000 + $100,000) / 20 percent = $1,000,000

Take a moment and calculate your desired net profit margin now and write it down.

My desired net profit margin is: _____

### Markup

Now that you've found all of your major expenses, you can correctly determine how much you need to mark up your services to make enough money to support yourself and your business. You need to determine an accurate markup number that incorporates every line item of your expenses, from your overhead to your personal salary. To understand how important this is, we recommend reading *Profit First for Contractors,* by Shawn

Van Dyke.

If you are pricing appropriately, your margin (which is your gross profit percentage), your overhead, and your expenses will all get covered under the umbrella of your markup percentage. We use markup to make sure the business has a cushion so that you can make payroll on time every time.

❖ A / B = Markup
❖ Total Sales / Cost of Goods = Markup

Here's what this looks like for ABC Home Builder:

❖ $1,000,000 / $800,000 = 1.25 (125%)

Take a moment and calculate your markup now and write it down.

My markup is: _____

Congratulations, you now know your numbers. However, it's not quite time to dance around in the endzone and celebrate just yet, as there is still one more important financial concept that you need to understand: *cash flow projections*.

## KNOW YOUR CASH FLOW PROJECTIONS

*Another aspect of leveling up your financial planning is running cash flow projections so that you always have enough money in the bank to pay your bills on time. Many custom home builders struggle with this, since expenses don't always line up with when money comes in from a long-term project. And for some businesses, cash flow can be even more unpredictable. (If the phone stops ringing out of the blue one month and you go through a slow time, it can affect your ability to cover your overhead costs.) If you're struggling with cash flow, talk with your SBGP coach. They can help you run projections for your business and better plan for expenses.*

# PROJECT RECONCILIATIONS

To verify that you are on track for your desired profitability, you should examine how accurate your estimates are compared with numbers you actually achieve.

To run a reconciliation, simply compare your estimate or quoted price with how much it actually cost when the project was completed. This enables you to determine whether you've made the amount you expected on a specific project. We have a helpful downloadable template for this on our website: drilldownlevelup.com/resources.

You can use your reconciliation numbers to make future adjustments to the markup you used for the project.

We help our clients with these exercises all the time, and they are often shocked that they aren't taking home as much as they intended. Recently, we worked with a custom home builder who was struggling with profitability, even though they were sure they had a 16 percent markup. They were great at watching their gross margin percentages but were seeing them decline slowly over about two years—even though their markup was consistent.

After doing a few reconciliations of their past projects, we found that they were only getting 12 percent. They were routinely losing about 4 percentage points of their markup because it cost them more to do the work than they realized. Some of the costs had become higher than expected, and other expenses were simply not accounted for when the initial estimate was made. In fact, they had some very big projects where the gross profit margin ended up only being around 10 percent. They were not billing for change orders or being diligent in following up with their subcontractors. When subs would take their sweet time sending invoices for projects months and months after they closed, it was much too late for the home builder to bill the clients.

These kinds of small errors can slowly sabotage your business if left unchecked. For this particular business, a 4 percentage point markup loss at $2 million per year was $80,000. Let me repeat that: They had $80,000 just slipping through their fingers each year. That's why it's essential to get into the rhythm of doing reconciliations for each and every job. Make it a consistent part of your operations. That way, you catch mistakes quickly so you can avoid making them again on future jobs.

For projects that go on for many months, you should set milestones throughout the timeline and do reconciliations a couple of times during the project to make sure you're on track. While you may not be able to adjust anything on a current project to improve profitability, you will at least be able to pinpoint where your numbers were off. If you wait until the end of a one-year project to do the reconciliation, you're likely to forget where certain expenses were higher, or why.

It's OK if you aren't able to calculate all of this data right away because you aren't tracking these numbers yet. Now that you know what you need to track, you can begin doing it.

Keep in mind that just because you should know all of your numbers doesn't mean it's your job to be the accountant for your business. There is a difference between knowing how your numbers impact your bottom line and tracking every single expense and invoice yourself. Leave the heavy lifting to your accountant or bookkeeper, but make sure that you understand the strategy behind how these numbers influence your profitability.

If you recently started working with an SBGP coach, don't worry about calculating your numbers just yet. Your coach will help answer any questions you have and will be there to walk you through each step of the process. Remember, our coaches have done this hundreds of times for talented business owners across the country, so you can rest easy knowing that you are in capable hands.

## A NEW PATH FORWARD

Business finance is a broad topic, and there is a lot to learn. Our goal with this chapter isn't to try to teach you everything you could possibly know. But we do hope that we've given you a solid

CHRIS PENASA

foundation that enables you to better understand the numbers behind your business and the story those numbers tell.

If you've never used your financial data to the extent we described in this chapter, you might feel like a whole new world of possibility has opened for you. Maybe you were driving an old junky car, and now you have a new vehicle with a speedometer, gas gauge, and windshield wipers. You were getting by without those tools before, but now you realize how much better life is when you have them. The data you glean from using financial data can help you make strategic decisions that have the power to change the trajectory of your business. If you haven't been breaking even, now you know how to fix it. If you realize your profit margin isn't as high as you thought, you know what to do to adjust it. This knowledge might seem like a small thing, but it can be everything for a small business.

We encourage you to keep leaning into your financial data as you work on evolving your business. You'll be amazed where it can take you.

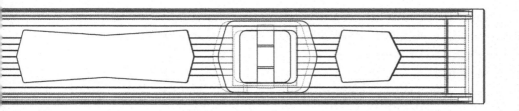

# CHAPTER 12

## PAINLESS PLANNING

As a business owner, you're definitely going somewhere. But the question is, Are you headed in the direction you want to go?

Now that we've walked through all of the major areas in your business to focus on to kick-start your growth, it's time to solidify your plans for how to move forward. Chances are you already have a pretty good idea of the kind of projects and initiatives that would make the biggest difference in your business. In fact, you might have identified so many opportunities for improvement that it's tricky to know where to start. That's where planning comes into play.

Although it might be tempting to get to work ASAP on a couple of things you already know how to do, you will have better results if you're strategic about your plans and prioritize your efforts. We recommend starting with the big picture to develop a clear vision for where you're going. From there, you can work backward to flesh out the details.

### CREATE SMART GOALS

All plans stem from goals. So before we go any further, let's talk about how to create good goals. The thought of setting the right goals for your business can be daunting, but the process doesn't have to be overwhelming. We recommend being SMART.

| | Attribute | Description |
|---|---|---|
| S | Specific | Define what you want to achieve in your business. Explain what, why, who, where, and when. The more specific, the easier it will be to reach because success will be clearly defined. |
| M | Measurable | Describe how you will track progress and measure the results of your goal. Good goal statements answer the questions: How much or how many? How will I know when I achieve my goal? |
| A | Attainable | The goal should stretch you out of your normal comfort zone but must be achievable, and you must believe that it is achievable. State why you know you can and will achieve it. |
| R | Relevant | Describe how the goal will be rewarding either by making something positive happen or by avoiding something negative. |
| T | Time Specific | Your goal must have a deadline. Without a commitment to a date, goals often die. State when you will complete your goal. |

## SAMPLE GOALS

The desired outcome: This company wants to increase revenue this year.

Here are examples of both good and poorly stated goals.

|  | Goal | Analysis |
|---|---|---|
| ✗ | We will increase revenue. | The goal isn't specific or measurable. Are they going to increase by $0.01 or by $1,000,000? |
| ✗ | We will increase revenue by 100 percent by Q2. | While the goal is specific, measurable, and time specific, it is likely not attainable. Unless they start with a very small amount of revenue, growing by 100 percent is extremely difficult, especially in a short period of time. |
| ✗ | We will interview last year's clients to see what we could do better. | While this might be a relevant goal for increasing client happiness in the future, it likely won't help with increasing revenue this year. |
| ✓ | We will increase revenue by 10 percent measured by year-over-year results on 12/31. | This is specific, measurable, attainable, relevant, and time based. |

Keep this in mind as you move on to the next section, where you will create annual and quarterly SMART goals. Don't let the specifics scare you. No one has a crystal ball to determine exactly how things will end up. Not hitting your goals exactly on the head doesn't mean your business will come crashing to the ground. But the fact that you put the time and effort into creating SMART goals will be immensely helpful in making the right kind of progress.

# FILL OUT YOUR STRATEGIC PLAN

To help you with your planning initiatives, we've developed a strategic plan template to record and track key information. In this chapter, we'll walk you through some examples to show you how to fill out your own plan. Make sure you visit drilldownlevelup.com/resources to download a blank copy of the template so that you can follow along and enter your own information.

## VISION

The first tab is Vision, which is all about the foundation of your business. This is where you record your core values, purpose, and more. You'll notice that the SWOT (strengths, weaknesses, opportunities, and threats) analysis is front and center, which is smart for long-term planning. (SWOT analysis was invented in the 1960s by a management consultant named Albert Humphrey at the Stanford Research Institute.) Finally, there is a section for objectives in four areas: financial, people, operations, and personal. This is where you fill in details on how you want the company to grow over time. For example, how big do you want to be? How much revenue would you like to make? How would your personal life change as your company grows? Getting all of this information in one spot will help you stay organized.

Sometimes owners get nervous at this point in the planning process because they are afraid to commit to specific long-term objectives. They have a vision for the future, but it might be a little fuzzy. If this resonates with you, know that you are not alone. It's OK if you don't know exactly how big you want the company to be, or if you want to retire in about 15 or 20 years. What's important is having a general sense of the direction you want go. That way, you can at least tell if you're pointed in the right direction.

You should also know that it's not uncommon to work toward a certain goal only to achieve some success and realize that you want to go another direction. Maybe you thought you wanted to have a bigger team, but you realized you actually just want to increase your profitability. If your vision shifts over time, don't stress it. You just want to recognize when that happens so you can course correct and stay on track.

Although you might not update the Vision tab of your strategic plan all that often after you first create it, we recommend that you review it regularly as a reminder of your big-picture goals. The biggest reason for this is you might sometimes find that your business is growing and making money, but you're veering away from actions that support your long-term objectives. Maybe you got caught in a reactionary mode and accidentally veered away from your vision. This document can help you hold yourself accountable for staying on track with growing in the way that is most meaningful to you.

## SBGP Vision ABC Builder

| Vision |
|---|

**Core Values**

**Excellence Always:** *We relentlessly pursue perfection. We are never satisfied with the status quo. Quality is everyone's job. We take pride in what we do and how we do it.*

**Respect for All:** *We cast a positive shadow on others. We leave things better than how we found them. We are gracious, empathetic, and kind.*

**All-In:** *Our customers come first. We are committed, not interested. We have grit (guts, resilience, initiative, tenacity). Be here now.*

**Team First:** *We are open and honest with ourselves and with others. We act with integrity at all times. We are accountable for our actions, consciously choosing to be part of the solution, not part of the problem.*

**Purpose/Your Why Statement**

*Building the dreams of lifelong customers*

**Key Focus/Sweet Spot**

*Exceeding expectations in all phases of constructing high-end ($500,000-plus) custom homes*

**Key Result Areas**

*Move into development*
*Grow leadership team*
*Expand geographic reach*

## SWOT Analysis

| Strengths | Weaknesses | Opportunities | Threats |
|---|---|---|---|
| Custom home building | Marketing | Economy is growing | Lumber and material costs |
| Sales process | Project management | Trend for move-up home buyers | Industry is booming; difficult to get subs committed |
| Home design | No backup subs | Richmond, Virginia, population growth | Interest rates increase |
| Local reputation | Financial profitability | | Finding quality employees |

### SWOT Results

Develop marketing plan, including target market, core messaging, website, and social media

Identify list of backup subs

Implement Buildertrend for project management and client tracking

Add material escalation clause in contracts

Develop financial model and implement pricing markup

## Long-Term Objectives

| Financial | People | Operations | Personal |
|---|---|---|---|
| Revenue $5 million in 2026 | Owner | Sales pipeline 8 prospects | Owner works 30 hours per week |
| Net Profit $500,000 in 2026 | Operations Manager | Build pipeline 3 | Exit strategy in place for 2031 |
| Free Cash Flow $250,000 | Sales Manager | Projects in progress 3 | |
| Six lots for future building paid in full | Office Manager | Buildertrend | |
| | Project Managers (2) | Marketing plan | |
| | Estimator | Website | |
| | Site Supervisors (2) | Social media | |
| | Office/Marketing Coordinator | Primary and backup subs | |

## ANNUAL PLAN

Now that you've defined your big-picture vision and identified some milestone achievements for the years ahead, you can figure out what you and your team will work on this year. To complete the annual plan, we recommend sitting down with your leadership team, as well as any other key team members, and brainstorming together on what your plans might look like.

Good goals to set for the year might relate to the number of projects you want to do, the amount of revenue you want to make, or the net profits you want to achieve. You should also think about things that get in the way of reaching your long-term vision and build a plan around addressing those issues. For example, you might need to implement new project management software to get better organized before you increase your volume. Or you might need to hire a marketing person so you can step out of those responsibilities and focus on other work.

Start by recording an individual goal and then break it down from there to come up with strategies and actions to reach that goal. Make sure you assign an owner and set a timeline for each one. From there, you can come up with KPIs that will let your team know you are on track to reach each goal.

## SBGP Annual Plan ABC Builder

| Annual Plan | | | | | |
| Goals | Strategies | Actions | Quarter Due | Owner | KPIs |
|---|---|---|---|---|---|
| Increase revenue to $2.5 million in 2021 | Complete 10 homes | Forecast projects and timing | Q4 | | Completed homes |
| Improve GPM to 20 percent in 2021 | Implement markup for job pricing | Review financial model; determine markup factor for all estimates | Q1 | | Job GPM |
| | Implement job | Review all jobs on completion | Q1 | | On budget |
| Free cash available of $100,000 by 12/31/2021 | Improve AR collections process | Reduce AR > 90 days from $100,000 to $0 | Q2 | | AR Aging |
| | Consistent Invoicing | Send invoices on the 15th and 30th of the month | Q1 | | |
| Average 10 new leads each month | Develop marketing plan | Build marketing plan, target market, core messaging, | Q2 | | New leads |
| | Refresh website | Engage web developer | Q3 | | Contract with developer |
| | Produce weekly social media posts | Define schedule and content | Q2 | | Schedule met |
| Develop sales pipeline of five projects each month | Track prospects | Implement lead tracking; find CRM? | Q2 | | Sales conversion; proposal turnaround time |
| | Develop sales process | Document existing sales process; review sales processes | Q2 | | |
| | Reduce proposal turnaround time | Identify biggest obstacles | Q2 | | |
| Average four projects in Progress each month | Improve sales close rate | Implement sales process | Q2 | | Sales conversion |
| Improve lead tracking, sourcing, estimating, project management | Implement Buildertrend | Implement and train for Buildertrend | Q3 | | Project tracking |
| Reduce risk with subs | Develop backup sub list | Identify subs with most issues and develop backup list | Q1 | | Sub list |

Next, you will input your data on your annual budget. There are three sections, but for the purposes of this template, you update the top-two sections (Previous Year Actuals and Current Year Budget) when you first fill out the form, and you keep the third section (Current Year Actuals) updated on a quarterly basis. (The tracker is formatted so that your totals automatically add up in the right column.) This serves as a handy financial snapshot for your business, and makes it easy to see how you're doing compared with your goals, as well as your performance from the previous year.

## Annual Budget

| Previous Year Actuals | Q1 | Q2 | Q3 | Q4 | Total |
|---|---|---|---|---|---|
| Revenue | $1,959,245 | $2,398,565 | $3,268,752 | $2,518,035 | $10,144,597 |
| Gross Profit | $422,080 | $474,230 | $608,715 | $458,155 | $1,963,180 |
| Gross Margin | 21.54% | 19.77% | 18.62% | 18.19% | 19.35% |
| Net Profit | $181,333 | $208,514 | $362,785 | $224,315 | $976,947 |
| Net Profit Margin | 9.26% | 8.69% | 11.10% | 8.91% | 9.63% |

| Current Year Budget | Q1 | Q2 | Q3 | Q4 | Total |
|---|---|---|---|---|---|
| Revenue | $1,850,000 | $2,485,000 | $3,650,000 | $2,820,000 | $10,805,000 |
| Gross Profit | $525,000 | $565,000 | $790,000 | $645,000 | $2,525,000 |
| Gross Margin | 28.38% | 22.74% | 21.64% | 22.87% | 23.37% |
| Net Profit | $190,000 | $310,000 | $440,000 | $290,000 | $1,230,000 |
| Net Profit Margin | 10.27% | 12.47% | 12.05% | 10.28% | 11.38% |

| Current Year Actuals | Q1 | Q2 | Q3 | Q4 | Total |
|---|---|---|---|---|---|
| Revenue | $1 | $1 | $1 | $1 | $4 |
| Gross Profit | $1 | $1 | $1 | $1 | $4 |
| Gross Margin | 100.00% | 100.00% | 100.00% | 100.00% | 100.00% |
| Net Profit | $1 | $1 | $1 | $1 | $4 |
| Net Profit Margin | 100.00% | 100.00% | 100.00% | 100.00% | 100.00% |

## QUARTERLY PLAN

After you complete your annual plan, you need to break it down by quarter. To do this, you will prioritize your annual goals, ideally spacing them out evenly so that the amount of work is steady throughout the year. At SBGP, we call these quarterly goals "rocks," which comes from Stephen Covey's book, *The 7 Habits of Highly Effective People*. The theory is that if you get the big things done—the rocks—then everything else will fall into place. Copy and paste your yearly goals from the Annual Plan into the Rocks section of the Quarterly Plan. This will make it easy for you to reference exactly what should happen at any point throughout the year.

# COMMUNICATE WITH THE TEAM

It's important to involve your team members in the planning process to make sure everyone is on the same page with how and why you are working toward common goals. This makes a huge difference in gaining your colleagues' buy-in on their work. One of our clients is a great example of this. Chris Caskey and Daryl Wendlick are the owners of Arrow Millwork in Greendale, Wisconsin. A number of years ago, they were running into issues with their 15-plus-person team. Most of the employees worked at their factory making cabinets for kitchens and baths. Everyone was busy, but production wasn't running as smoothly or efficiently as they would have liked.

As Chris and Daryl began to get more strategic on how to improve production, they created new processes and goals, and shared their new expectations with the team. They thought they were communicating what employees needed to know, but that ended up not being the case.

Their team felt that management was expecting more and more from them for no clear reason. And when the team was tasked with higher goals, it wasn't always possible to meet them because they didn't have the right internal systems in place. Team members would rush to get their individual parts done, but then the department handoffs would get bottlenecked. No one understood how the whole production process fit together, so they didn't know exactly what their colleagues needed or how to help them. Morale was low, and people blamed each other for anything that went wrong.

Chris and Daryl realized that all these issues were stemming from a lack of communication on general business planning. They needed to involve their whole team in the planning process to give them the big-picture view of where the company was going. So they sat down with the whole team and explained the yearly goals. From there, they backed into each one, making sure employees understood all the little steps that would help them reach their goals.

Almost instantly, the attitudes of their team members completely changed. A light went on for them in terms of where the company was going and why, and they knew how their own work fit into that vision. From there, the production team provided Chris and Daryl with a ton of insightful ideas on how to make even more improvements to their processes and systems. Together, they figured out what caused issues and how to easily solve them. One quick win was that they rearranged the production floor to get things moving in a more systematic way. This change alone eliminated the confusion around handoffs and made it easier for workers to collaborate.

Fast-forward a couple of years, and Arrow Millwork has found a strong rhythm in making planning a team sport. Everyone in the company is well informed on company-wide goals, as well as goals for individual job functions. They've seen what a big difference it makes to get everyone on the same page, and their organization is doing better than ever.

## PLAN TO EVOLVE AND ADAPT

A lot of owners need to have a mindset shift when it comes to planning. We aren't chiseling plans into stone, where the finality of those plans can cause a lot of anxiety. Instead, we're using a pencil and eraser because part of the plan is that things will probably change. When a business grows and needs to evolve, planning should be dynamic. Owners and their teams need to check progress regularly and adapt as needed.

Even loosely made plans are much better than not having any plans at all. You wouldn't just start building a house without a blueprint. You don't want to build a business that way either.

For more support on assessing and implementing strategic plans in your business, speak with your SBGP coach.

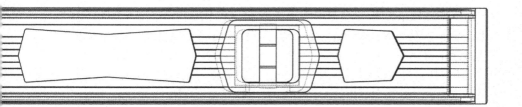

# CHAPTER 13

## CONTINUOUS IMPROVEMENT

A vid readers of business books or personal development books learn valuable information that inspires them, and they realize they have the power to change the course of their life and business. Sometimes people follow through with new actions and spark a lifelong transformation, but, more often than not, they fail to take it from theory into practice.

Most of us have the best intentions when it comes to driving our own personal development, but it's easy to get distracted. We might begin to implement some new best practices, but then an employee quits, and then there's a problem with a client's project, and then a personal issue pops up at home. Before we know it, that amazing book we read is just something that gathers dust on a shelf.

Do not let that happen with this book. We all know how life has a way of constantly testing our bandwidth. Making time and space to focus on the concepts in this book will take hard work, but we promise you that it will be worth it. We've worked with hundreds of business owners over the years, and we have seen firsthand how the information in this book has helped them create a totally new reality. This can be your experience as well—if you commit to implementing what you learned.

It all starts with creating new habits. As we've previously discussed, to drive lasting change, you need rhythm and consistency. You need to do the same things over and over and get comfortable with them. Otherwise, taking the necessary actions is never going to feel natural. It's just like having a gym membership. If you go several times a week, it becomes easy because you get into a routine. You show up without giving it much thought, you work out, and you get on with your day. In fact, exercise can become so engrained in your life and schedule that if you have to skip a session, you feel like you're missing something because it throws off your internal rhythm and routine. But if you only go to the gym once every couple of weeks (or less), it feels like a big deal, and you have to practically drag yourself there. The workout disrupts your routine, and it might even add stress to your life trying to fit it in. To make matters worse, when you're working out, it feels hard because you're out of shape.

You can think about your business the same way. It is critical to get into a rhythm where you're spending time on the things that matter most. Instead of getting derailed and constantly pulled back into working *in* the business, you need to be intentional about working *on* the business. We promise you, creating this kind of consistency is half the battle when it comes to the evolution of your business. If you can establish an ongoing practice of putting focus on all the important things that need to be done, continuous improvement will become ingrained in the culture of your company.

## HAVE ACCOUNTABILITY

Just the word "accountability" has the power to make some people cringe. It can have a negative connotation, like you might get in trouble if you don't do something. That's why it often gets a bad rap. People assume that it's a mechanism to combat laziness, or that hardworking individuals shouldn't need to be held accountable to get things done.

We want you to acknowledge all of the negative feelings you might have around accountability. Now take a deep breath and release them. Accountability is your friend. In fact, it might actually be one of your best friends, since it always has your best interest at heart.

The thing about accountability that people don't realize is that missing goals and deadlines is not always a negative thing. We've yet to meet a business owner who sits around twiddling their thumbs, so if they aren't getting certain things done there's a good reason for it. Exploring the "why" behind the gap between intentions and reality can provide a lot of helpful information and allow for troubleshooting.

For example, if a goal was missed because the owner didn't have time to work on a particular project or task, there is likely a problem somewhere else in the business. (Is the company short-staffed? Do employees or subcontractors need more training? Do certain roles and responsibilities have to come off the owner's plate? Is there a need for a better system or process to free up the owner's time? Or is the goal too big and needs to be broken down into bite-size pieces?) The sooner we can address these kinds of issues, the better.

People also tend to put off tasks that intimidate them. If they aren't sure how to do something, they avoid it. The answer to this might be simple, such as more research needing to be done before the task can be completed. Adding that preliminary action step can work wonders for unblocking progress. That's why having consistent, short-term goals and check-ins is the name of the game for both self-accountability and team accountability.

## CREATE A WEEKLY SCORECARD

We created a simple way to track your progress and many of your KPIs. The weekly scorecard is a spreadsheet that consolidates the most important data for your business. Each metric has a target goal and a person assigned to it. We recommend that every employee be responsible for at least one KPI. Once everyone understands what's expected of them, it's as simple as adding each week's numbers to the scorecard to track progress. The whole team reviews the scorecard together in a weekly meeting, which adds a layer of accountability for inputting numbers on time and helps keep everyone on the same page business-wise.

If your business is currently more of a "solopreneurship," you should schedule time each week to fill out your scorecard and review the results. We highly recommend determining how to add a layer of accountability to this process so you don't procrastinate calculating your weekly numbers. Consider enlisting the support of a mentor, coach, or assistant to check in with you about your numbers.

The scorecard is helpful for identifying issues in real time. For example, if you don't have enough new leads coming in right now, you're at risk of falling short of many other goals that are tied to leads down the road. This knowledge enables you to act quickly and address current issues to change your trajectory.

When you track your data over time, the trends are important as well. You can see whether you're improving, stagnating, or falling behind in various aspects of the business. This includes seasonality once you get a years' worth of historical data on paper. If you and your team are working hard on the right projects, your numbers will show it, which provides a little extra encouragement. When you're easily reaching or surpassing certain metrics on a regular basis, you can think about increasing your goals.

We included a sample scorecard on the next page, keeping in mind that each business is different, and what's important to track in one business will not necessarily be the same for others. You can go to drilldownlevelup.com/resources and download a blank version of the weekly scorecard that you can customize for your business. Also note that if you are an

SBGP coaching client, we will help you come up with your target numbers and build them into your personal scorecard. If you hit your target number for a KPI, the cell for that week will automatically turn green. If you're a little off, it will turn yellow; and if you're too far off, it will turn red. Color coding the data each week makes it much easier to spot problem areas at a glance, and it also helps you recognize trends. Having a couple weeks in red or yellow is to be expected, but you want the columns trending to a greater proportion of green.

| Category | KPI/Metric | GOAL | FREQUENCY | 4-Jan | 11-Jan | 18-Jan | 25-Jan |
|---|---|---|---|---|---|---|---|
| Mkt | # New mtgs with referral source | 2 | weekly | 1 | 2 | 2 | 3 |
| Mkt | Community events (9 quarterly) | 9 | quarterly | 0 | 2 | 2 | 0 |
| Mkt | Social media posts | 2 | weekly | 2 | 2 | 2 | 2 |
| Sales | Currrent # of prospects | 4 | weekly | 3 | 3 | 4 | 4 |
| Sales | Dollar value of prospects | 2M | weekly | $1,600,000 | $1,600,000 | $2,100,000 | $2,100,000 |
| Sales | # of qualified leads | 10 | weekly | 5 | 7 | 9 | 10 |
| Sales | # of qualified lead follow-ups | 1.5 | weekly | 1 | 0 | 2 | 2 |
| Sales | # of new leads | 1 | weekly | 1 | 2 | 1 | 1 |
| Operations | # of projects under construction | 5 | weekly | 5 | 5 | 5 | 5 |
| Operations | Avg days behind schedule | 0 | weekly | 1 | 1 | 0 | 0 |
| Operations | Avg days above budget | 0 | weekly | 0 | 0 | 0 | 0 |
| Financial | Total cash on hand | $80,000 | weekly | $90,000 | $105,000 | $88,000 | $93,000 |
| Financial | Monthly revenue | $500,000 | monthly | | | | $535,000 |

# FACILITATE PRODUCTIVE MEETINGS

We've all been in meetings that have been a total waste of time. People weren't prepared, the discussion wasn't focused, and nothing was accomplished. It's a no-brainer that you shouldn't waste your time (or anyone else's) in unproductive meetings, but avoiding this common pitfall is harder than it seems. To ensure meetings are well worth the time invested in them, you need a solid structure that ties discussion topics to actions and accountability.

We use a template for regular check-in meetings, and we always recommend that our clients do the same. Having weekly meetings is a best practice for keeping everyone on the same page with what's going on in various parts of the business. Maybe it's a weekly production meeting with the operations team and/or project management team. Maybe it's a weekly check-in with your office staff, who also help with marketing and sales support. Whatever the structure of your business, you should get your team together on a regular basis to communicate. You can use the meeting agenda template to make sure you stay on track. With a clear structure on what to discuss, you'll find that people don't go off on tangents, and key meeting objectives are not accidentally missed.

## HERE'S HOW IT WORKS:

❖ **Business/personal update**: Every meeting starts with a quick check-in. Keep it positive and hold space for your team to share some quick updates on how they're doing—either personally or within their role at the company. People can share any recent achievements or wins they've had with clients. SBGP team meetings are always on Mondays, so we start with a weekend update.

❖ **Scorecard**: Here's where the scorecard comes into play in your meetings. You only need to go over it in detail once a week to review the new data, but you should keep it front and center in every meeting. This helps you focus everyone's efforts toward the KPIs and metrics that matter most. If everything is on track in your scorecard (green), there's no need to have a lot of conversation. But if there are issues (yellow and red), you might need to add an action item to the list.

❖ **Rock review/quarterly objectives:** Next, talk about the major things you're focusing on this quarter. (Pull this information from your strategic plan [see chapter 12].) How are you doing? Are things on track?

❖ **Action item list:** Go through the previous week's action items and confirm that everything was finished as planned. If there's a next step, or if the task is not complete, add it to the New Action Item section. (If things keep showing up on the action item list and progress isn't being made, then have a conversation about it.)

❖ **Ongoing projects (review monthly):** The next section of the agenda is flexible in terms of the content. For example, reviewing financials monthly makes a lot of sense, and this is a reminder to do so.

❖ **Issues list:** This is where your team talks about any problems that might be cropping up—internally or with client projects. It's important to get these on everyone's radar sooner rather than later so you can address things early and course correct. During the meeting, prioritize the items on the issues list from most critical to nice-to-solve. Be sure to address the most critical items either through assigning a next step that goes in the new action item list or resolving it during the meeting.

❖ **New action item list (to be reviewed in the next meeting):** Use this section to record all of the action items that have been identified in the meeting. Specifically identify who is doing what by when and the priority level of each task.

The meeting agenda template takes a little work to build out for the first recurring meeting, but after that, it becomes much easier because you're continually talking about many of the same things and sharing status updates. In fact, you should *always use the previous meeting's agenda to create the new one.* You simply move the "new action items (to be reviewed in the next meeting)" up into the action items section.

As the business owner, ideally you should delegate the management of the meeting agenda to someone else. That person creates the new agenda each week (retaining the previous week's action items), takes notes during the meeting, and shares the agenda with everyone afterward.

# MEETING AGENDA

| Business: | ABC Home Builder | Date: | 11/9/21 | Day: | Tuesday |
|---|---|---|---|---|---|
| Client: | Joe Builder | Time: | 9:00 ET | | |

## Business/Personal Update

Everything seems to be going the way it should. Rhythm is a little bit better. Brenda starts full time next week. Need to create a job description. She'll be working four 10-hour days. Will be onsite inventorying trucks, running errands.

## Scorecard

| | KPI | Comments |
|---|---|---|
| 1 | Review Weekly Scorcard | Done. Everything is on track |

## Rock Review/Quarterly Objectives

| | Rock | Who | Priority | % Complete | Comments |
|---|---|---|---|---|---|
| 1 | Two home starts. | Sam | 2 | 50% | Second home will start before the end of the quarter. |
| 2 | Complete marketing/education videos—three (heating, ventilation, passive solar). | Sam | 3 | 75.00% | Passive and heating are done. Need to do ventilation. |
| 3 | Raise supervision fee by 1% | Sam | 1 | 100.00% | Done |
| 4 | Add in official handoff process at the beginning of projects. | Sam | 4 | 25.00% | Will do it before the end of the quarter. |
| 5 | Create document for our involvement in the design process—clarify roles and responsibilities. | Sam | 5 | 25.00% | Need to schedule meeting with designer |
| 6 | | | | | |

## Action Item List  Goal = At least 90% of List Completed

| | Actions | Who | Status | Priority | Comments |
|---|---|---|---|---|---|
| 1 | Schedule post-mortem for Smith project. | Sam | 1 | 2 | Will bring in trade partners to review what went well or didn't. Schedule. |
| 2 | Write bullet points for Efficiency page on website. | Sam | 0 | | Specifications and process are usually the areas that need tweaking. Move to next week. |
| 3 | Create format for meeting with project manager (training/progress). | Sam | 1 | 3 | Format is working great. |
| 4 | Schedule job site visits with two framers who want additional work. | Sam | 1 | 1 | Did visit with one, very happy with him. Okay not meeting with a second framer. |
| 5 | Firm up date for next open house. | Sam | 1 | 1 | Done. |
| 6 | | | | | |
| 7 | | | | | |
| 8 | | | | | |
| | | | 80% | % Completed | |

## Ongoing Projects—Review Monthly

| Project | Who | Status | Priority | Comments |
|---|---|---|---|---|
| Review marketing schedule—previous month/current month. | | | | |
| Review financials monthly (mid-month) and cash flow forecast. | | | | |
| | | | | |

## Issues List

Impact = High, Medium, Low  
Urgency = High, Medium, Low

| | Issue | Who | Impact | Urgency | Comments |
|---|---|---|---|---|---|
| 1 | Still need to develop a framing crew. | | | | |
| 2 | How to keep the balance between SOPs/structure and openness to innovate. | | | | |
| 3 | How to space out work better to avoid overload. | | | | |
| 4 | When to hire the next employee. | | | | |
| 5 | | | | | |
| 6 | | | | | |
| 7 | | | | | |

## New Action Item List (to be reviewed in next session)

| | Actions | Who | Status | Priority | Comments |
|---|---|---|---|---|---|
| 1 | Add to sales process—gather pertinent info and pause to take a week to consider if it is the right fit/timing for us. | Sam | | 2 | |
| 2 | Write bullet points for efficiency page on website. | Sam | | | |
| 3 | Add net profit line in cash flow spreadsheet. | Sam | | | |
| 4 | Add to sales process asking about interior designer. | Sam | | | |
| 5 | Create agenda for Smith postmortem. Send invites. | Sam | | 3 | |
| 6 | Create job description for Brenda's position. | Sam | | 1 | |
| 7 | Schedule videographer for ventilation video. | Sam | | | |

Download a blank version of the meeting agenda template from our website: *drilldownlevelup.com/resources.*

## STAY FOCUSED ON THE BIG PICTURE

Whether you're in your 90s or your 20s, you should think about your transition plan. How will your time in the business end? Sometimes our clients are surprised when we ask them to figure out what will happen decades from now, but it's important to consider. Without this long-term vision, you can't focus on the kinds of improvements you'll need to make in your business to reach your desired end point. (If you want to keep your transition plan a mystery to your team members for now, that's fine, but it shouldn't be a mystery to you.)

Is your goal to create a job for yourself or a long-term business? It might feel like you have a business, but you're really just working a job—without the benefits of having someone else provide your health insurance, vacation days, pension, 401K contribution, paid parental leave, and any of the other good things that employees enjoy.

That's why you are on the pathway from what is essentially freelance work to having a thriving business, which is a valuable entity on its own. This provides you with the option to have passive income from your company—where you make money without trading your time. You can also work toward selling the business for a profit or passing it down to the next generation. All of these options are better than just turning off the lights and walking away when you're done.

**Profitability:** As you focus on the big picture and work toward your transition plan, a key area to hone in on is profitability. Small-business owners often think that higher profitability will come later, and that's OK. They'll continue working hard, and eventually it will all work out. We love the optimism here, but we implore you to add a greater sense of urgency. Profitability needs to be a key focus *now.* You don't want to wait to make more money. In addition to the obvious reason that you have bills to pay now, don't forget the power of investing your money. With compounding interest, money grows over time. If you start investing a portion of your profits now versus 10 years from now, you could be in a very different spot by the time you want to retire. Another key thing to consider is that if you want to ultimately sell your business for an impressive sum, it needs to be profitable well before then.

Give yourself a refresh on the financial chapters in this book (chapter 3 and chapter 11) and come back to them regularly as needed. For many business owners, improving profitability is the initial top priority because it makes everything else easier. It takes the pressure off them, enabling them to focus on other work that matters. Wouldn't it be more productive (and fun) to work on developing your marketing and sales strategies once you knew each and every project that you completed was delivering you a consistent profit?

**Leadership**: Everything we've covered in this book comes back to leadership. If you want your business to change, you need to change. Instead of just focusing on the present, you need to always look toward the future. Everything you're doing today should support the outcomes you want tomorrow, next week, and 20 years from now. Becoming more strategic and intentional can be challenging, but gets easier with practice.

One of our clients, Scott Kennard of Wentworth Builders, is an excellent example of how a leader can evolve and transform his business. When we first started working with Scott two and half years ago, he had lost his spark. He always delivered incredible work, and his reputation was second to none. However, his company struggled in a few areas, and he was beyond tired of trying to get his team to do what they needed to do. After 20 years in business, he was no longer enjoying being a builder.

We worked with Scott on every topic in this book. He met with a coach every two weeks, just putting one foot in front of the other to make progress. Sure enough, things started to turn around. One of his biggest improvements was gaining clarity on the company's mission, core values, and culture.

From there, he began measuring everything against these key elements of the business. Employees learned exactly what was expected of them and why, and performance did a 180-degree turn for the better. Scott continued plugging along, developing systems and processes that improved how work got done. Profitability went way up, the company started bringing in more of their preferred ideal clients, and Scott found a renewed sense of joy and fulfillment. These days, he's focusing on developing the team so when he's ready to retire, he has options. By getting the business in such great working order now, he knows his successor will be well positioned to take over when the time comes.

## BUSINESS HEALTH ASSESSMENT

Before you started chapter 1, we asked you to fill out the Business Health Assessment to set a baseline on where you were at that point in time. The assessment should have also helped you identify some initial priorities for what you might want to focus on next when it comes to evolving your business.

Now that you've completed the book and you're beginning to work on action items for your business, the assessment is a handy tool for helping you prioritize the work ahead of you. (If you're a new SBGP coaching client, you'll fill out a more comprehensive version of this assessment.)

Don't get overwhelmed here. If there are many things you want to work on, start by picking a few of them. Or even better, start with just one. Even if you take baby steps, you'll make progress that will add up over time.

Set a calendar reminder to retake the assessment every six months. Not only will it help you stay on track for working on what matters most, but you'll also be able to see how far you've come. This is a helpful trick for staying motivated and keeping up your momentum.

## YOU GOT THIS

Business growth is challenging, so don't let yourself get discouraged. Success is built sequentially. You do one thing at a time, putting one foot in front of the other. Chunk down your goals so you don't get overwhelmed, and work at a pace that's comfortable to you. (This is how you build or remodel a house. Apply the same mentality to your business.) Remember that this is a marathon, not a sprint. You got this!

# STAY CONNECTED

At Small Business Growth Partners, our goal is to help business owners in the construction and trade industries have thriving, fulfilling businesses. Whether you work with us or not, we hope you take this book to heart. Use the resources below and create the business you want.

- ❖ **Resources:** All of the downloadable resources mentioned throughout this book are available on our website: drilldownlevelup.com/resources. We believe in these tools, but they won't do you any good if you don't actually use them. Please take the time to download these resources to ensure you get as much as you can out of this book.

- ❖ **Next steps:** We love working directly with small-business owners in the construction and trade industries. Coaching people and helping them improve their life and business is what lights us up every single day. If you liked this book and are not yet an SBGP coaching client, please see if you are eligible to become one by going to our website for more information. We also have many articles, e-books, and blog posts that you might find helpful. We can't wait to get to know you better soon!

# ACKNOWLEDGMENTS

Even though this book was penned under my name, many extremely talented people were involved in creating and organizing its contents—from our incredible team of coaches to our hardworking, dedicated, and incredible clients. Carolyn Turner, our Chief Coaching Officer, is one of the most caring, passionate, and gifted business coaches I have ever met, and has made our coaching system and client results what they are today.

My parents, Rudolph and Nancy Penasa, were instrumental in building my work ethic through many hard years in retail, and they never stopped believing in me.

I'd also like to thank Amelia Forczak and the Pithy Wordsmithery team for the invaluable assistance in the creation of this book.

Finally, I'd like to acknowledge and thank my partner, Terry Elton, for all of his help in building this incredible company and putting our concepts and methodologies into this book. Over the years, we have helped so many builders, contractors, and trade businesses achieve success beyond their wildest dreams, and I know this book will help us contribute even more. Terry, you are my best friend, and without you this journey would not have been nearly as enjoyable. Your friendship, skills, and guidance have made my life purposeful and filled with joy.

# ABOUT
# SMALL BUSINESS
# GROWTH PARTNERS

Small Business Growth Partners (SBGP) is a private, specialized coaching firm for construction and trade businesses that was started by Chris Penasa and Terry Elton. After deciding a better, more effective growth model was needed specifically for builders, remodelers, and trade companies, Chris and Terry came up with their unique model to cater to this industry's needs. Specifically, they wanted to help small-business owners get their life back through increased sales, profitability, consistency, and team engagement. With a specialized team of full-time (non-1099) coaches that focus 100 percent of their time and effort on coaching, Chris and Terry and SBGP are now creating the impact they first envisioned. As of the first printing of this book, SBGP operates in—and is the most utilized and trusted business coaching company—in 16 states.